THE KABBALAH OF FOOD

THE

KABBALAH

OF

FOOD

Conscious Eating
for Physical, Emotional,
and Spiritual Health

RABBI NILTON BONDER

SHAMBHALA
Boston & London
1998

SHAMBHALA PUBLICATIONS, INC.
HORTICULTURAL HALL
300 MASSACHUSETTS AVENUE
BOSTON, MASSACHUSETTS 02115
HTTP://WWW.SHAMBHALA.COM

Printed in the United States of America

♾ This edition is printed on acid-free paper that meets the American
National Standards Institute Z39.48 Standard.

Distributed in the United States by Random House, Inc.,
and in Canada by Random House of Canada Ltd

Library of Congress Cataloging-in-Publication Data

Bonder, Nilton.
[Dieta do rabino. English]
The Kabbalah of food: conscious eating for physical,
emotional, and spiritual health / Nilton Bonder.
p. cm.
Includes bibliographical references.
ISBN 1-59030-331-8
1. Weight loss—Religious aspects—Judaism. 2. Food—Religious
aspects—Judaism. 3. Health—Religious aspects—Judaism.
4. Spiritual life—Judaism. I. Title.
RM222.2.B617 1998
296.3'68—dc21 97-42940
CIP

To Pedro Soibelman
to whom life was like cooking:

"If you mean to make a casserole and it overcooks . . .
no problem—it becomes a stew.
If it still overcooks,
we can always turn it into a pot roast!"

Contents

C O N T E N T S

Introduction

IN THE BEGINNING
WAS THE MOUTH

Defining who the Jews are, ethnically and socially, is one of the great conundrums of our time. One solution might be to say that the Jews are an oral people. Their tradition points to that truth by virtue of what leaves the mouth (words) as well as what enters it (food). Just look at Jewish history: the word is their major source of artistic production, and indeed they are known as the People of the Book. Even their God is one who creates by means of the word. In addition, wherever Jews have settled or passed through, they have ravenously adopted and creatively adapted the seasonings of that place, producing a vast and varied cuisine: there is Yemenite, Moroccan, Polish, Russian, Italian, Spanish, German, and American Jewish food. The Jewish menu probably contains traces of every cuisine the Jews ever had enough time to taste.

The world of ritual also provides evidence. Jewish religious rites frequently coincide with special foods for each special occasion. The pace of the Sabbath is determined by its three meals, and its main blessings make reference to the act of eating. Yom Kippur, the Day of Atonement—the holiest day of the religious calendar—is marked by fasting and then the festive breaking of the fast at the day's conclusion. Passover, the second most celebrated festival, turns food into a symbolic language in such a way that the Haggadah, the holiday liturgy, could be easily mistaken for a menu.

The Jewish people's fondness for food is famous and much parodied. The stereotypical Jewish mother urging "Eat, eat!" is matched only by the Italian mother in a Mediterranean contest to see who can stuff their children's bellies with more love. Such attachment to food is very revealing and makes one wonder: How can this orally fixated people presume to advise anyone on avoiding the pitfalls of wrong eating and contribute to the worldwide effort to the cure obesity? Judging by the silhouette of the typical rabbi today, it would seem that they cannot. Far from being role models for health or attractiveness, they seem to believe that one has to weigh a lot in order to "carry weight" in this world.

Yet, in the past, the rabbinical sages themselves were the ones who developed a complete theory and practice of eating, based on two assumptions: (1) the almost cosmic importance attributed to food and (2) the shape of the physical body as a complex expression of meanings.

Regarding the first assumption, for the rabbis obesity has little to do with the concept of thinness versus fatness but instead is a matter of lightness versus heaviness. In this book, "obesity" thus refers to heaviness on several different levels, and the "diet" used to treat it is not a food-limiting regimen but a means of becoming lighter. As we shall see, the rabbis are masters of dieting in this sense.

The phenomenon of chronic overweight among Jews, associated as it is with specific conditions of Jewish history, can teach us a great deal about the nature of obesity itself. The following story illustrates the relationship between the historical process of a people and that of an individual.

The Baal Shem Tov (known as the Besht) once beheld in a dream the one who in future would be his neighbor in paradise. After waking from the dream he decided to go and meet this saintly person and stay with him for a few days. To his surprise, the fellow turned out to be a very fat and seemingly coarse person. "How well can a man disguise himself?" the Besht thought to himself. He was certain his host must lead a double life. Probably he got up every night and accomplished God knows what virtuous deeds in secret. But no—the man slept deeply all night long. He woke up early, hastily said his prayers, and sat down to a lavish breakfast. He ate even more at lunch and three times as much for dinner. And this he did consistently for several days.

"Let's wait for the Sabbath," thought the Besht. Maybe his neighbor's holiness would coincide with that of the seventh day. But he was wrong once again: his host ate and slept even more than he did during the work week. Unable to restrain his curiosity any longer, the Besht said, "I had a question in mind when I first came here. But I have another one now: Why do you eat so much?"

"I'll tell you why," said the neighbor. "It all has to do with my father, who was a good man and a good Jew, very gentle and fragile. His only worry was how to please his Creator. Nothing else was of concern to him, neither money nor honors, nor even his own health. He lived only by and for the Torah. One day, on the way to the synagogue, bandits attacked him and tied him to a tree. He was ordered to deny the Lord. This he emphatically refused to do. He was then ruthlessly beaten, but went on refusing to comply. They eventually poured kerosene all over his body and set him on fire. My poor father was so weak and thin that he flared up at once and burnt for only a short while. And I, who witnessed it all, swore that if I were ever to undergo such a test someday,

I would not let them dispose of me so easily. I would show them that a Jew does not just burn up like a meager and miserable candle. No! When I burn, I will burn for such a long time that they will die of hatred. And that's the reason why I eat so much—why all my energy, all my passion, is devoted to food. Not that I feel hungry, you understand. . . ."

This story depicts that condition in which one is ready to devour whatever obstacles are in the way. Much of the time, when we eat, we do it for reasons other than hunger. We eat to prove something, to express something, to avoid something, to control something, to repress something. Often we feel so powerless in our lives that the best way we can find to communicate with the outer world is through the most concrete form of exchange with it. In contrast to our breath, which is involuntary, our food intake is something over which we have absolute control.

So the act of eating frequently has a wider meaning than merely the literal intake of food. The above story points to how intensely people can project feelings of various kinds onto their eating habits (and even onto their own physique). A talmudic saying asserts that one can judge a person's character by "his cup, his pocket,

and his anger" (in Hebrew, a play on words: *kosso,
kisso,* and *ka'aso*). These three refer to the most common worlds of exchange between human beings and the
universe. The cup stands for drink and food, or the general category of our substantial exchange with the universe. The pocket represents money or, more broadly,
our power relationships with the world, while anger has
to do with the way we deal with negative emotions.
There might be some short circuits among these three
worlds, which sometimes merge together in interrela-
tionship. In the story of the Besht, for example, the
realms of the cup and anger merge.

The rabbis therefore present us with "diets," and
not with reducing regimens, in order to deal with these
issues as deep, complex systems instead of just controlling calories. Herein the reader will find insights based
on the Jewish tradition, which has speculated on and
transmitted knowledge about the mysteries of dieting
and food symbolism for millennia. It is a tradition that
draws on its traumas in order to gain wisdom about the
problem of obesity.

Based on holistic knowledge, the rabbis' diet considers obese those who are unsatisfied when relating to
food and health on the physical, emotional, social, or
spiritual planes. It also aims at alerting us against two
special kinds of obesity, which the rabbis take very se-
riously: ecological or moral obesity and political obe-

sity. In this book we will look not only at the teachings, experiences, and suggestions of several masters from different periods, but also at the insights of the *Shulḥan Arukh*, a sixteenth-century rabbinical treatise, which we shall read in an updated, practical way so as to discover the secrets of the rabbis' diet.

1

THE KABBALAH OF
FOOD

The Art of Receiving

The word *kabbalah* can be literally translated as "receiving." According to rabbinical tradition, understanding the meaning of "receiving" and being able to live it is a sacred art to be practiced and perfected over a lifetime.

An old legend contrasts the two seas of Canaan: the Sea of Galilee, abounding with living creatures, and the Dead Sea, a brew of inanimate matter supporting no trace of life whatsoever. What is the reason for this difference? When the Sea of Galilee receives the melting snows from the Golan Heights, it allows them to flow in turn into the Jordan River, from which they stream down into the Dead Sea. But the Dead Sea, instead of letting these waters go, holds on to them, for it does not know how to receive.

Receiving means establishing a relationship with

nature or the universe in which we live. If we understand "receiving" as a one-sided phenomenon—with the emphasis exclusively on what *we* are going to get out of this partnership—then we gradually draw away from this relationship of exchange, which ultimately represents *life*. The Dead Sea is as much a sea as is its brother, the Sea of Galilee. Yet it is deprived of that subtle vitality which results from the art of receiving, which can only be fulfilled by letting go of what has been given.

To know how to receive, then, we must learn to set up an exchange process with the universe around us, which in turn absorbs us into the ecological chain that nourishes us.

All the pain, anguish, and anxiety inherent in the "receptive" (i.e., kabbalistic) life network originates in the problems that we have with receiving. Like the Dead Sea, we frequently fail to strike a balance between the sweet and salty waters (or *kar/ham*, cold/warm—a kind of Jewish *yin/yang*). An abnormal situation results, a state of excess in which nothing flows. We cannot empty our vessel of its waters, and so we become progressively filled with a sea of tears.

This principle applies notably to the realm of food, where merely receiving is not an aim in itself: that is, eating is not the end of a process, but rather the beginning of one, without which there can be no receiving in the true sense. Physically the body is formed in the manner of the Sea of Galilee, as reflected in this morning blessing of Jewish prayer:

> Blessed are You, our God, King of the universe, Who fashioned human beings with wisdom and created within them many openings and cavities. It is obvious and known before Your Throne of Glory that if but one of them were to be ruptured open or blocked, it would be impossible to survive and to stand before You. Blessed are You, O God, Who heals all flesh and acts through wonderful deeds.[1]

In order to be healthy, we must keep the bodily openings at both ends clear: both those that take in and those that let out. This prayer therefore reminds us every day to be aware of life as a continuous exchange. Notice that according to this holistic concept of receiving, every interacting element is necessarily an inseparable part of the whole.

Contemporary Kabbalists draw on the phenomenon of electrical resistance to help us understand this concept of receiving. To produce an electrical event such as the light in a bulb, two things are required: (1) electrons must flow through the wire, and (2) there must be some resistance to this flow. Without flow or resistance, light will not appear in the bulb. Living beings, like the light bulb, are not energy themselves; they are energy *vessels* (resistances). When energy from the original Source passes through the "resistance" of life, it is converted into the phenomenon of existence.

Depending on what living creature it infuses, a particular energy can turn into speech or a roar, a leap or a thought, fear or pleasure. Being is itself a phenomenon originating in the harmonious interaction of energies within an individual and the way and the extent to which the flow of such energies keeps going. Mostly we are aware of the influx of energy and of the resulting effect on ourselves, and we forget about the continuity of the flow, which is definitely an integral part of the harmonious operation called *health*.

In human beings, much of the incoming energy is converted into *consciousness*. In order to go on leading a healthy life, we must be in harmony with the continuity of flow that such production of consciousness brings on. Nowadays we understand that ecological problems and the destruction of the environment are mostly a consequence of such discordance. The problem of "obesity" fits into this same category.

Culture, technology, and social relations are the products of an exchange with the world based on the transformation of energy into consciousness. Such phenomena are relatively recent and bring about complex

changes that have a great impact, particularly where
food is concerned. Until human beings developed consciousness as such, their relationship to food was controlled by instinct, just as it is with other animals. This
instinct in turn was the information provided by a long
chain of interactions with life itself. It represented the
result of successful evolutionary processes that provided creatures with the necessary information to maintain healthy exchanges with the world, allowing for
survival.

Having become conscious and living in a milieu
fabricated by this very consciousness, human beings
can subvert their instincts and the exchange balance at
any time. The list of foods on our menu is elaborated
not from an ecological-geoclimatic appropriateness to
the energy flow, but from a complex civilizing influence.
A Brazilian who is offered Chinese food cannot make a
nutritional decision purely out of intuition. As a conscious being he must determine whether such food is
suitable for him; whether he may have already eaten
something else that might not agree with this new food;
whether there is any consideration of climate; whether
this food is compatible with his activities before and
after eating it; and so on. So we have to compensate
for the handicap of our deactivated instincts with the
awareness—a conscious process—of what is healthy
and what is not healthy. Although we can certainly work

to restore our instincts to some extent, the complexity of reality will sooner or later require consciousness to play a role in our decision making about what we eat.

Following a diet means learning how to receive. And in order to receive, we need an efficient form of resistance. On the one hand, we depend on inbred qualities such as intuition and common sense. On the other hand, we depend on elements acquired through the development of consciousness and culture. These latter two elements are, in fact, nothing but the surface of profound interactions between life and its environment that human beings have come to master through tradition and science.

In other words, for human beings, the art of receiving food entails components unusual to the animal process. Intuition is not in itself an effective guide to diet. Nowadays, receiving from a healthy exchange such as the one performed by the Sea of Galilee has to do—in regard to human beings—with culture, science, religion, and politics. The Jews had a term for this aspect of enlightened intuition: *kashrut,* which means the state of being kosher. This is the corrective application acting to compensate for whatever might be lacking in one's instinct.

The consequence of not knowing how to receive through food—namely, "fat" or excess—has implications beyond physical disease or obesity. It is a situation of imbalance that leads to "obesity" of the moral, emotional, and spiritual sort. For all conscious beings, then, who wish to understand and fine-tune their relationship with the universe, it becomes necessary to follow an outer code in each and every exchange, so as to ensure some healthy receiving. If this does not take place, one will pay the price of finding oneself disconnected from the flow of life. In the words of Hosea (13:6):

> When they were sated, they grew haughty; and so they forgot Me. . . .

The Four Worlds of Food

According to the Kabbalah, when the universe was created, there was an outpouring of Divine Energy in the form of primordial Light. Because the "vessels," or metaphysical amphorae, into which this energy was poured could not withstand the intensity and purity of the flow, they progressively broke, one by one, into smithereens. This event, known as the shattering of the vessels, is responsible for the scattering of sparks of Divinity into Creation. Extracting these sparks from worldly things and elevating them back to their Source is seen as the main task for human beings.

It's not surprising that such a disaster occurred, for receiving is a process not to be suppressed. According to this creation story, the shards resulting from this irrepressible event brought into being the universe of attributes, things, and phenomena. Human consciousness itself may be likened to an overflowing vessel, unable to contain the colossal flow of energy that is available to it, whether in the form of knowledge, creativity, love, or other manifestations of the Divine Light. It nevertheless retains some of this flow, which is the source of any insights into the world or the self that come to us.

Let us consider this kabbalistic description as it applies to the world of nutrition, in which the vital energy of the food we eat must be received and allowed to flow through our system. Receiving it in the wrong way brings on some physical symptom, which is a sign from our body, emotions, and spirit that something is wrong. This is the yellow caution light that appears before the onset of illness. The ailment brought on by receiving something in a bad way becomes manifest on different levels. On a physical level, it may appear as pain, an ulcer, a blemish, or perhaps a bad odor. On an emotional level, it takes the form of sleep and nervous system disturbances. And on a spiritual level, it manifests as negativity, depression, and destructive impulses.

All such problems are of course interconnected.

By ignoring our discomfort or dulling our sensations with drugs, we can at best dim the yellow light. That will not prevent the emotional or spiritual symptoms of sickness from arising on other levels. It only means it will be harder to identify the disease once every single level has symptoms of its own.

Kabbalah speaks of four worlds corresponding to different levels or dimensions of reality, thus expanding our concept of health and nutrition far beyond the physical or even emotional and mental planes. Within this concept, a fourth element is the world of Emanation (Atzilut). This is the world from which energy flows across the upper worlds and empties into the material world, the world of Action (Asiyyah). The fourth world is therefore the point of origin for the flow of vital energy coming from the Divine Source. This flow in turn is stored on the spiritual plane, which allows it to enter the mental plane, which in turn supplies the emotional plane. Finally, from the emotional level the flow is conducted to the physical plane, fueling the body for action and exchange, a phenomenon known as existence.

If the world of Emanation alone were the conveyor of all flows of energy, the law of exchange would be subverted. According to the Kabbalah, the energy flow goes both ways, returning from the physical, material world to the One that is the pure source of all energy.

The Kabbalah sees all forms of exchange among

living beings and the environment, including eating, in
terms of an interactive process among different worlds.
Such a process links earth and heaven, matter and energy, action and intention. Living beings are responsible as intermediaries between these realms, as long as
their inner or existential world is centered exactly
where heaven and earth meet. Regarding this inner
world, the Talmud states: "This is the world where
heaven and earth kiss."

To help clarify this abstract concept, let us look at
a famous story from the Talmud that alerts us to the
danger of studying the subtleties of the Kabbalah before
achieving a certain degree of maturity. The story tells
of four sages who go for a walk in the *pardes*. This Hebrew word encompasses a double meaning here. When
translated literally, it means "orchard." But when the
word is treated as an acronym, PRDS,[2] each of the letters offers some interpretation for disclosing the secrets
of the Scriptures and of the world itself. The word
pardes is thus composed of four others:

P = *peshat* = literal
R = *remez*   = allusive or analytical
D = *derash* = symbolic
S = *sod*   = secretive

In the course of their stroll, the four sages contact the
four dimensions of understanding the reality of ex-

change between the outer and inner universes. Through the total interaction of all four dimensions, the impact of the revelations of the secretive orchard causes the sages to suffer in different ways. One of them goes mad, the second one dies, the third one abandons his religious faith, and only the last one, Rabbi Akiva, manages to make it through the orchard safely.

Leaving the orchard as a deranged person means being unable to distinguish between the literal, allusive, symbolic, and secretive realities outside its limits, to such an extent that the individual is no longer functional. Dying signifies the loss of one's individual identity. Leaving the place as a heretic means having a wrong understanding of the relationship between the different dimensions. The one who leaves unharmed is he who can negotiate all four worlds along an inner path, in a harmonious manner that allows for a true exchange between the individual and the universe. Rabbi Akiva is the only one who returns to the functional world, thus being able to act concretely and perpetuate the cycle of exchange, by making use of his life experience or insights.

Leaving the orchard intact means not succumbing to disease, maintaining one's physical functioning even within the most ordinary reality. It means leading a healthy life, without allowing the body, intellect, psyche, and spirit to get sick from the process of life and exchange. Being able to stroll easily through the orchard means *being* in the broadest possible way: "receiving" from the original flow of divine energy and allowing it to be channeled through one's unique individuality and through the world of actions and historical events.

It is exactly from such safe walks through the orchard that the world harvests fruit. It is up to each and every individual to stroll in that world of exchange and meaning and to be able to bring about fruition. It is what we all manage to bring safely from the world of interaction that allows for a *shulḥan arukh*[3]—a "laid table," offering the most exquisite banquet of possibilities in life.

The kabbalistic interpretation of exchanging and receiving presupposes a nutritional understanding. Table 1 offers a concrete example of such interpretation, which classifies fruits according to their capability of receiving. The different physical structures of fruit end up representing the different worlds. The fruit's rind (*kelippah,* plural *kelippot:* often translated as "husks" or "shells") represents some hindrance to the flow of energy and, as a consequence, to our ability to receive it from eating the fruit.

Rabbi Ḥayyim Vital,[4] a great Kabbalist of the seventeenth century, used such everyday magical objects as fruits as examples to show how all things could

Table 1
FOOD SYMBOLISM IN THE FOUR WORLDS

World	Interpretation Level	Reality	Food Symbolism	Fruit	Illness or Disorder
Physical ASIYYAH Structural World	KATUV The text itself; parchment and ink with which it is written	Salts and minerals	—	Inedible Peels and pits	Nausea Vomiting Digestive problems Constipation Diarrhea
ASIYYAH Functional World	PESHAT Literal	BODY Vegetal & animal	Material exchange Hunger/ appetite	Highly defended	Obesity Anorexia Lack of fitness
YETZIRAH World of Formation	REMEZ Allusive	FEELINGS Peel or husk	Ritual-symbolic Manna/ hallah Haroset	Defended	Psychosomatic illness Gallstones Glandular problems Allergies Ulcers

BERIAH World of Creation	DERASH Symbolic	MIND Pit	Collective unconscious (mystical/ psychic) *Matzah*	Poorly defended	Serious receiving problems Cardiac obstructions & arrests Unbalanced cells Cancers
ATZILUT World of Emanation	SOD Secret	SPIRIT	Fasting Faith	Surrendered	Karmic interference KARET (being cut off from the universal flow) Mutations affecting descendants

be understood, in relationship to the notion of receiving and exchange, as manifestations of the four worlds. According to him, fruits are divided into four different categories: highly defended, defended, poorly defended, and surrendered. (Table 1 shows five different worlds instead of four, because the material world, Asiyyah, has been divided into two subsections in order to better explain this analogy.)

As stated by Rabbi Vital, the highest possible level assumed by a fruit as a manifestation of Atzilut, the world of emanation, is the state of being absolutely edible. The Atzilut world permeates the essence of certain fruits in such a way that they reproduce the insubstantial, spiritual nature of that world. In other words, being absolutely edible turns them into nonfruits, ready to lose their identity and become a part of whatever creature consumes them. They are unconditionally surrendered, without any sort of protective husk, whether outer (rind or peel) or inner (pit), as in the case of strawberries, figs, and mulberries. It is true that some of these are outfitted with a fine skin protecting their flesh, for it would be impossible otherwise to maintain their shape and separate existence in a limitless universe. But although these fruits preserve their identity with the help of some kind of physical boundary, they do not use their skins to defend themselves against the external world. Such a fruit represents the possibility of existing without any protection whatsoever, whether we are talking about the physical protection of skin or the mental defense of ideological or rational structures. This fruit's nature is secretive, but not because it is defensive; to the contrary, it does not allow itself to be limited by a husk or by any need other than the truth. Its commitment to the absolute turns it into a manifestation of reality that is hidden from most of us, and therefore it is seen as belonging to a secret dimension.

The world of Beriah, Creation, is in turn more densely expressed within the material world. Since this world of Creation is close to the subtle level of Emanation (Atzilut), its manifestation in the form of fruit does not result in resistance or defense against the outer world. Fruits of this type therefore do not grow outer rinds, yet they still need protection in order to safeguard their identity, their original energy. Their defenses are revealed, not in an absolute way, but around their cores. These fruits, although they do not have rinds, do develop inedible pits, which represent what we are calling a poorly defended state. Peaches, plums, dates, and olives are typical examples of this category of fruits that are not well defended yet are less ready to surrender their flesh.

In the realm of interpretation, these fruits may be compared to symbols and metaphors. In that realm, absolute understanding contracts so as to conform to mental and psychological conventions and standards. Nevertheless, the symbolic world is not completely "defended," and its essence is not solely dependent on forms. Its form-free nature is due to its openness to interpretation, although there is always some impediment (husks) to understanding created by ideological bias or conventional mental concepts.

In the world of Yetzirah (Formation), the need for a definitive shape in order to maintain integrity becomes more and more urgent. Here fruits develop a well-outlined and assertive contour. Their inedible rinds are purely a manifestation of their dependence on form and of the defense of such form against the outer world. Nevertheless, the little influence they still preserve of more subtle levels allows their core to be defenseless. Protecting themselves from outside threats with the help of a tough rind is enough. The core is still relatively soft and edible. Walnuts, coconuts, and pineapples are excellent examples here.

This is the world of feeling, where the heart itself remains free and open while at the same time having to be confined within certain structures. Open-hearted feelings such as love, kinship, and friendship are, on the one hand, manifestations of an attitude of surrender; on the other hand, they must be contained within extremely well-defined structures. For example, love is imprisoned within the goal of reproduction (form); friendship is imprisoned within the need for solidarity in order to survive; and so forth. Thus, as strange as it may sound, feelings are both free and enslaved. That is the reason why civilization, even though it values feelings for their honesty (like the open, pitted core of a fruit), also warns us of the danger of fully surrendering to our feelings unless they are limited by outer structures (rinds or husks). Free at heart and limited only by external rinds, this level manifests itself in interpretation through allusion. Allusion may at first seem like free association, but in reality it turns out to be limited by patterns and external structures.

Peels and pits, or any other kind of protection, are not an abnormality but simply a manifestation. An abnormality might originate as an exacerbation of such manifestations, which are merely a consequence of existing in all the different worlds at once. Kabbalists called these defense mechanisms kelippot, and they represent the boundaries that come into existence as the various worlds manifest themselves on the physical level. The intellect needs protection in the "heart" in order to be permeable ("edible") to the outer world, and it therefore does not develop a shell. Feeling, by contrast, does need an "edible," free, and fluid heart as well as protection from the world, as its essence is by nature passionate and biased. Kelippot are most certainly limitations, but they are not negative or bad. In a differentiated world, the limits that restrain or impede us from doing a thing are the very ones that allow for its existence. For example, peeling a pineapple might be a laborious process, but were it not for its rind, this fruit would be too vulnerable, and we would not have a chance to enjoy it.

As we turn to the world of Asiyyah, the physical and most concrete world, fruits take a very defended form. They therefore develop inedible peels and pits. Mangoes, avocados, and papayas exemplify this world. Representing the structural world and its urge for strict definitions in both outer boundaries and inner core, Asiyyah becomes, in its most radical manifestation, absolutely inedible. These fruits—in which the generosity of the universe is no longer expressed—are utterly defended. They exist exclusively for their pre-established reproductive tasks, which define them as fruits. But they do not offer themselves in any way. Here the intensity of kelippot, the need to define, separate, and protect, is at an absurd extreme. Any openness represents a firm threat to order. This is a literalistic world where the dictatorship of structures and functionalities is ruthless. The kelippah is so intense that every one of its elements has to be defended, protected, and closed.

The manifestation of the four worlds in the realm of fruit resembles manifestations of human experiences in the orchard. As with fruit, so with people, who can be seen to have similar kelippot. There are those who develop a hard, impenetrable core in their hearts, hampering the give and take of energy; they become "obese" in their hearts, owing to their habit of grasping at the energy that they receive and not sharing it. There are also those who develop a hard outer shell, inhibiting the continuity of the receiving flow on another plane. These people also fatten up and become obese.

Diseases of any sort have to do with either the overgrowth or reduction of such defenses. These defenses are natural manifestations of the four worlds expressed on the gross level of matter and are to be preserved in that condition as defenses and not as "diseases." The Jewish morning blessing previously quoted—in which we ask that bodily organs which are either open or closed remain that way—is an acknowledgment that having too many or not enough kelippot can both be hazardous to our health.

In the world of Asiyyah, when the channels of receiving become closed, we are faced with starvation or anorexia. When the channels of giving become closed, we are faced with obesity. Health depends on the appropriateness of our defenses in either retaining or letting go.

In the allusive dimension of Yetzirah, problems with our ability to receive manifest themselves in an indirect, nonliteral way. Retention and excessive loss do not have immediate consequences here; they proceed gradually. In contrast to the world of Asiyyah—where inedible or indigestible substances cause immediate closure of what should be open (constipation, gas, nausea) or openness of what should be closed (diarrhea, vomiting)—in the world of Yetzirah closure evolves with time. For example, whatever was open might close down because of excessive calcium, thus creating calculi, or solid deposits in various organs. Closure in this world is also responsible for allergies, blisters, asthma, and bronchitis. If, in Yetzirah, what was closed becomes open, the result can be ulcers, emphysema, or lesions of various kinds. These are most commonly disorders originating in the existence of "peels but no pits." In other words, such problems originate in the outer kelippot or in the organs belonging to structures dealing directly with the outer world, such as digestive or respiratory systems and the epidermis.

Within the symbolic world of Beriah, disorders of receiving are even more indirect and subtle. In this case, when an opening shuts down, we are dealing with kelippot or blockages in the circulatory system, thus generating cardiac arrests. When what should be closed opens up, then we have strokes or cellular leakages that cause all kinds of cancer. Beriah is the realm of the mind, where management of the major bodily functions is centered, and where disorders have a structural impact on the organism. There are neither peels nor shells here. Undesirable closures or openings take place not in organs that regulate our relationship with the outer world, but internally. Defenses causing cardiac arrests act like "pits" in the heart, in the same way that "pits" in the cells are responsible for tumors. The origin of such disorders is either blockage or disruption of balance in managerial organs, in this case the heart or the cells.

Atzilut is a world in which disorders transcend the individual. They manifest as a genetic mutation affecting not merely one individual but all subsequent generations, leaving a karmic impact in the form of consequences that transcends one's life span. Mutation is a malfunction of something that presents neither "peel" nor "pit," for the DNA consists of pure information, unlimited by any kelippah or defense. Thus the corresponding illness is not an opening of what is closed or a closing down of what is open in the concrete sense, but in a subtle one. Opening up to some destructive information or closing down to constructive information is what becomes, on this level, a disease. The spirit, being the very connection between our physical entity and the essence of life, becomes sick to the extent that this connection is weakened.

Of course, the ancient teachings of Judaism do not

speak in terms of modern scientific concepts like mutation and evolution. Instead, Judaism sees spiritual diseases that involve neither peel nor pit as causing
karet—the state of being disconnected in the deepest
possible way from the universal flow. This biblical concept is usually translated as "excision" and means
being cut off from one's people, that is, from one's spiritual source. It is considered the worst of all punish-
ments, even worse than capital punishment. And that is
why the individual becomes an outcast, excluded from
the collective task in life. Karet is the price paid for
wrong receiving that has a karmic impact. It is a disor-
der of the spiritual plane. This is in fact the worst
human nightmare, for it means the failure to live one's
true life purpose and, even worse, a disconnection from
life itself. This kind of sickness has the potential not
only for the loss of health or even death but also for the
extinction of one's species. It is a sickness that transcends the individual and creates negative consequences on the collective level.

The fourth column in Table 1 refers to food symbolism. Jewish tradition assumes that both food and the
mouth are important means for conveying messages regarding the different worlds in relation to human needs.
The physical world of Asiyyah represents the primary
wishes of the body for strength and prosperity. The feeling world of Yetzirah represents the desire to live our

life at the right pace and thus find inner peace. In Beriah, the world of the mind and of structural management, we struggle to prevail over the destructive tendencies in our nature that threaten the continuity of the entire life process. And, responding to the wishes of the spirit, in the Atzilut world we seek to maintain the vital connection between everything that exists in the concrete world and the Source of all life.

In Asiyyah, food rituals are personal and vary with the individual. The body's desires for survival, well-being, and comfort are what matter here.

In Yetzirah, where the reality is that of feelings and the interpretative level is that of allusion, one finds examples such as *hallah* (the braided bread eaten on the Sabbath) and *haroset* (a mixture of chopped apples, nuts, cinnamon, and wine, served at the Passover seder). In both cases, food alludes to a collective situation and the emotions connected with it.

Hallah, for example, reminds us of the time when the Jewish people wandered in the desert after fleeing from slavery in Egypt. They survived thanks to a food called manna that, according to the Bible, was sent by God and poured down every weekday from the skies along with the dew. The two loaves of hallah customarily served on the Sabbath represent this manna, which appeared every morning in daily portions, but on Friday—the day preceding the Sabbath (the sacred day of rest), when gathering food would be forbidden—the manna came down in double portions. And so the bread served on the Sabbath reminds us that human beings should not only work for their daily sustenance but must also store food and take some rest.

As for ḥaroset, this symbolic food is consumed at the Passover seder, which commemorates the liberation from slavery in Egypt. Because of its reddish-brownish color, this dish resembles mortar, which reminds us of the oppression of the slave labor used for the construction of the pyramids.

In these two examples, feelings related to our need for rest and renewal and for freedom are symbolized through food. Feeding oneself within the world of feelings means providing for the satisfaction of emotional needs.

Within the mental Beriah world, food symbolism addresses questions of a structural order. In the first two worlds, we are concerned with the survival of either an individual or a group of individuals; now, in Beriah, we attend to the human species at large. Individual or societal questions have to do with a successful relationship with the environment. Survival and reproduction depend on finding the necessary resources in the relationship with the outer world. Regarding survival of the species, the inner traits of the species are what is at stake. Interference with inner traits might make the external project of survival unfeasible at either the individual or social level. When dealing with species, the concept of "eating" means nurturance from evolutionary moves that allow for better adaptation or, as in the case of malnutrition, developing traits that might lead to extinction.

Matzah, the unleavened bread that is a traditional ritual food for Passover, symbolizes this level; it pertains not merely to individuals or specific groups (such as the Jews) but to the human species as a whole. While the biblical story of Exodus unfolds in the specific setting of Egypt and around the confrontation between Moses and Pharaoh, the food symbolism points to a broader reality concerning these mystical and historical facts.

The Jews' escape from Egypt and Pharaoh's downfall take place in the Hebrew month of Nisan, which generally falls in April. Pharaoh can be interpreted as the Ram deity of Egypt, and this seems to be related to the paschal sacrifice of a lamb. This time of year coincides with the astrological sign Aries, the Ram, thus translating the confrontation between Pharaoh and the liberated people into a confrontation between the Ram (Aries) and the God of Israel. With this symbolism, we are transported from the arena of history into the realm of cosmic significance, in which the Ram as Aries reveals the universal dimension of this spiritual battle.

Notwithstanding, the rabbis asked themselves: What is so terrible about a poor ram that it should symbolize a war of cosmic proportions? And so they answered: When two rams are feeding, one of them always tries to drive the other away, using its horns as a weapon. The aggressor ram does this not because it wants to eat the other's portion, but merely in order to prevent the other ram from having what it has.

Cosmically, the ram represents the willfulness that causes us to desire something for ourselves alone, without caring about what others are going to get. On Passover, this self-will of ours actually engages in spiritual combat with the God of Israel, whereas in the functional world, as represented by Pharaoh harassing Israel, we have a historical manifestation.

In the nutritional realm, matzah engages in combat, so to speak, with *ḥametz* (leavening). According to the literal, Asiyyah level of interpretation, we are told that when the Jews hastily fled Egypt, there was no time for the bread to rise; thus, in the desert, unleavened bread became a symbol of that historical moment of freedom, and this is why we eat matzah and avoid ḥametz on Passover. But let us look at the inner reason, as symbolized in the spelling of these two cosmically opposed words. The Hebrew letters that make them up are somewhat similar, the only difference being that *matzah* (M-TZ-H) has the letter *heh* (H), while *ḥametz*

(H-M-TZ) uses the letter *ḥet* (H). Now, every letter in the Hebrew alphabet has a meaning associated with it. The letter *heh* stands for the name of God, whereas *ḥet* stands for sin. These two letters are very much alike in appearance. All you have to do is break the left side of the *ḥet* (ח) to turn it into a *heh* (ה). By breaking the will of this cosmic sin of wanting everything for oneself and not sharing with others, *ḥametz* is transformed into *matzah*. This continual spiritual battle, expressed in our inner universe at the Beriah level, is represented in this festival by the victory of the unleavened bread over the leavening.

In the spiritual Atzilut world, the symbolic representation is not food but fasting. Here our definition of *fast* is not "to abstain from eating," but "to actively feed oneself with nothing." Jewish tradition prescribes fasting on several special days, including Yom Kippur, the Day of Atonement, as well as days recalling catastrophic events of great injustice (such as the destruction of the Holy Temple, marked on Tisha b'Av) and times of crisis when the group faced the threat of extinction or genocide (as described in the Book of Esther). Fasting is a voluntary interruption of the nutritional mechanism and, in a way, it temporarily dismisses the game of life. What better way to symbolize the appeal to a last resort than to abstain from this major directive in life—the act of feeding oneself. Such an appeal is not uncommon in our time as a desperate attempt to exert influence in areas where there is otherwise no access whatsoever. When the government is not sympathetic to a cause, its proponents may stage a hunger strike in front of the White House in the hopes of getting some attention, even though they realize that one person's (or a group's) fasting is not what guides the political decisions of a nation.

This being the case, in the face of extinction, mutation, or karmic consequences, the only way to use food as an expression of the desire to reconnect with the life flow is to suspend the act of eating itself.

All the analogies developed here aim at showing that the food chain represents manifold bids to transcend merely physical survival. Food concretely expresses our exchanges and serves to manifest the distinct worlds of existence.

The idea of different, interpenetrating, and interacting worlds is essential to the receiving of mysteries, or Kabbalah. A broader awareness of reality and the ways in which it unfolds into different dimensions will uncover for us the art of seeing beyond, living beyond, and, eventually, feeding ourselves beyond the merely physical and sensory aspects of this act.

For the "diet" proposed here, it is essential to learn how to relate food symbolism in its several forms to the different levels I have previously explained. The major exercise is to identify either vitality or disease in one's food exchanges and to recognize how they relate to the four worlds. Thus, we must conduct our search for health not in one world alone but in all the different worlds combined. This might look like a rather complicated and endless process. And so it is, if we identify this process as a matter of *health*—a constant, integrated, and responsible interaction with the universe. On the other hand, it is a rather simple process, since all we have to do is live our lives fully; by doing so, we will be automatically engaged in the search for meaning and pleasure in health.

Three Attitudes toward Food

In an article entitled "Eating as an Act of Worship" (1982), Louis Jacobs classifies three different attitudes toward food: asceticism, puritanism, and acceptance with gratitude.

Asceticism regards abstinence as a virtue. The ideal is to reduce one's physical needs to the minimum required for survival. This perspective places fasting as the appropriate means to attain a holy state.

Puritanism similarly rejects physical pleasure as an end in itself, although it does not accept extreme self-denial. The appetite for food is understood as a necessary evil, instituted by the Creator to ensure our survival, rather than as something positive.

Acceptance with gratitude regards our physical appetite as a gift of God that is not at all shameful. Although it is not the highest human activity, eating does have the possibility of becoming a spiritual practice that leads to holiness.

In this view (mainly taught by the Hasidic masters),[5] the ingestion of food has to do with the Lurianic doctrine[6] that conceives of the universe as brimming with dispersed sparks of holiness that fell into the material world during the cosmic event known as the shattering of the vessels. The Kabbalah says that every bit of matter in existence contains these sparks, whose representation in the celestial worlds can be revealed by the letters naming that matter in one's world. It is as if the letters were some sort of molecular structure revealing secrets of other realities beyond the visible ones on that matter. In any event, the relevant concept here is that, as from the material configuration of food, one can effectively get to the source of Emanation, where energy originates.

When we eat, our thoughts should be more connected with God than at any other time, says Elias de Smyrna.[7] The source of this idea is found in the phrase "They saw God, and they ate and drank" (Exodus 24:11), interpreted as meaning that they intended to feel the presence of God in their hearts while eating and drinking. In other words, according to the Hasidim, two sacred intentions may be associated with food. The first intention is to survive and be strong in order to serve God. The second, higher intention is the difficult task of mentally elevating all the spiritual forces, the "sparks," that reside in food. These forces are well disguised beneath the concrete form they assume in the physical Asiyyah world, as seen in the case of fruits, which assume form, taste, and smell. Such manifestations in the concrete world are the very veils interposed between the pure, sheer energy of Creation and the individual who derives nourishment from them.

The *tzaddikim* (masters; singular *tzaddik*), however, have a deeper and keener understanding of reality. Their thoughts are always focused on elevating the sparks. The tzaddikim work to free the vitality contained in the sparks, imprisoned within husks that impede the flow of energy and thus prevent our receiving it. They therefore strive to free only the mature vital energies within a healthy receiving/exchange relationship. It is worth highlighting the importance of maturity as a condition allowing for a healthy flow of energy. The Bible states that fruits growing on a tree are not to be eaten or benefited from within the first three years after its planting (Leviticus 19:23). Such fruits are called *orlah* (first peel) and are not considered ripe. They contain immature vital energy, which can be extremely harmful to other living forms.

In Hasidism, this biblical concept is used to explain the mystical reasons for circumcision. The foreskin of the penis, which is removed in the Jewish ritual of circumcision, is called *orlah* in Hebrew. The Hasidim believe that this coincidence is no accident, as the penis is a channel for the semen, which is the major vital concentration of living energy in the human being. Semen is undoubtedly the channel for a powerful connection between heaven and earth. The ova certainly contain this living force, too, but the female reproductive cells remain inside the body and thus do not require the same kind of protection and care. The foreskin is thus a kelippah, a devilish device that seizes control of powerful vital forces before the full process of maturation has been completed. And that is the reason why this kelippah lodges exactly where the energy, or semen, becomes manifest. The danger is that, if the energy of the semen does not mature, *shedim* (little demons) will come to life. If fertilization takes place, however, the orlah phenomenon—the possibility of immature vital forces taking shape or starting to exist—is extinguished.

It is important to note that *satan*, the word for "devil" in Hebrew, has the same stem as the verb meaning "to impede," "to prevent." Thus, it literally represents a blockage to the connection with a healthy flow of energy, whereas kabbalah (receiving) is the exact opposite, allowing for a free flow of energy.

Regarding food in its most concrete aspect, the Berdichever Rabbi[8] differentiated between those who ate scantily and those who consumed their food with pleasure and delight. He said: "Although it is harder to keep holy thoughts in mind in the second case, one is undoubtedly far more rewarded." He knew that those who love to eat find it much more difficult to free themselves from this attachment and therefore have a harder time devoting themselves to holiness while eating. At the same time, these are the people who can experience what he calls "toiling for bread." In the first situation, however, individuals experience "bread with no effort," namely, a bread that does not offer them any growth through their consumption. The elevation of the sparks entails gathering them *down here*, on the most ordinary plane of reality, the world of pain and pleasure, and being able to transcend that plane by becoming a kind of holy envoy, channeling energy through the flow of life.

According to Rabbi Shneur Zalman of Liadi,[9] this mealtime battle between holiness and secularism is to be understood literally, for the Hebrew stem of the word for "bread" (L-H-M) is the same as the stem of the word for "battle" (M-L-H-M). Eating (like sex) is one of the most instinctive acts still preserved in our daily routine. Serious battles take place when we pursue the art of living in a holy (that is, an integrated) way. In accordance with this perspective, when we strive to achieve the right proportion of instinct and consciousness in every act of life, we are at the front of a daily battle in the depths of our being. The result of the battle is that we either elevate the sparks or allow them to fall even lower.

The possibility of extracting health from the daily act of eating not only on the physical but on all planes is as real as the possibility of generating sicknesses and disorders on all these planes. After all, this process involves not only health or disease but also habit, attitude, and intention. For the rabbis, there is no neutral ground when we're dealing with food: either we strengthen our lifelong habit patterns or we break away from them, and there is no room for compromise.

When sitting at the table, we face the possibility of accomplishing a holy act. It is up to us to make our food either healthy or not. Numerologists note that the Hebrew word *okhel* (food) has the same numerical value (57) as the value of the Tetragrammaton, the Divine name YHVH (26) added to the value of the word *El* (God; 31). When eating, one is receiving. If understood from its very origin, this "receiving" turns out to be itself the source of the flow. This flow has to do with the return of the sparks imprisoned in matter, and by bringing them out of exile we produce life, vitality, and health.

2

BAD HABITS

The Way Back from Exile—and Out of Habit

Exile is among the central myths of Judaism. In a literal sense, exile refers to events such as the expulsion of Adam and Eve from Paradise, captivity in Egypt and Babylon, and conquest by the Romans and others. In a more subtle sense it represents an absolute withdrawal from one's own nature. The end of exile, then, stands for a utopian, messianic time in which we return home, to our own nature and our own being.

Exile is less radical than assimilation or extinction, but it is nonetheless a severe experience of displacement that produces a profound sense of longing. Those who are in exile are constantly aware of where their *center* or home is. They feel out of place and anxious to find their way back. All their prayers and poems speak of the return, of a reencounter with the good old days.

Those who follow diets are aware of their exile, their withdrawal from the body. They live under the pressure and hope for a return to health and beauty. Reb Shlomo Carlebach[10] says that many people have addresses, but few live in true homes. For most people, bodies are nothing but "addresses," and few of us make ourselves at home inside them. Consciously or unconsciously, we dissociate, withdraw from the body, and yearn for a past condition when we felt at home. Not everyone had an aesthetically ideal body in the past, but most of us have experienced moments of well-being in a healthy exchange with life. The reconnection with the body-home is the way back from exile inside this body-address.

A problem arises, however, in that if we try to reach some ideal conception of our body, we will never arrive *home*. Even though our body may change, it is merely a change of address that has taken place. The Ugly Duckling never stopped feeling ugly until he realized his identity as a swan. He therefore grasped what the true way back to his body-home was. A human being also will stop being ugly when he or she becomes a beautiful swan and stops trying to be a pretty duckling, for this is not the ideal but the exile itself. Trying to be what they are not by pursuing an illusory aesthetic is what makes people turn to diets, which fail to correct the problems with receiving that led to obesity to begin with.

Hasidic rabbis speak of the danger of having one's

soul imprisoned in food, or being "exiled in food." They say that this vital energy trapped in food can only be freed with the help of a tzaddik who carries out a *tikkun* (a "repair" that puts an end to exile). This person can be seen as the inner tzaddik-master at the center of each of us, who guides us to a state of balance.

In the Jewish tradition, the "other side" (*sitra ahra*) is the address that takes over the home, thus assuming a demonic character. The term *satan*, also called Sitra Ahra, represents forces that distract and displace us from our inner master-center. As we have seen, the Hebrew word *satan* literally refers to obstacles or impediments. We fear being absolutely and irreversibly overcome by these demons. Yet, thanks to our memory of our true home, this does not actually happen. This very memory, on the other hand, is responsible for the experience of exile.

Body, Soul, and Intellect: Who Is the Impostor?

Al-Harizi, a Spanish Jewish poet and philosopher who lived in the twelfth to thirteenth centuries, posed this question: "In the dispute among body, soul, and intellect, who is the impostor?" In Al-Harizi's extended allegory, Heber ha-Keni is the character who personifies the constant fight between soul and body, each of which blames the other for his exile. According to this allegory, the intellect's function is to help the soul confront the body's desires and interests, for the soul finds itself at a disadvantage before the body's concrete and immediate demand to have its needs met. For human beings, it is the intellect, rather than the instincts, that lends consistency and concreteness to the demands of the soul. It thus enables the soul to concretely express its motivations and impulses with the help of reason.

In our time, this dispute seems to be coming to an end. The impostor has not been found, because there are no impostors. Soul, intellect, and body are all human tools of receiving. The soul is responsible for long-range exchanges and the body for exchanges of immediate needs, while the intellect mediates between the two. The intellect will sometimes take it upon itself to justify the body's needs to the soul and at other times to justify the needs of the soul to the body.

The intellect decodes what is received both from above (spiritually, by the soul) and from below (through the senses). When this decoder does not work harmoniously or healthily, the messages it ends up producing are either distorted or blocked, thus preventing the possibility of receiving. A physical act such as eating can thus be the result of the wrong receiving or wrong decoding of a message originating in the soul.

Once a sick man approached the Yud and asked him to pray for his health.[11] The Yud advised him to go see a certain man called Shalom who lived in a nearby village. Arriving there, the sick man found that the only person named Shalom was a drunkard who lived in a run-down shack on the outskirts of the village. He waited for Shalom to become sober and then requested his help. The drunkard asked him for a gallon of whiskey. After receiving it, Shalom advised the man to bathe in the river, for that would certainly cure him. And so it did.

When the man returned to the Yud, he asked him the reason for sending him to a drunkard. The Rabbi replied: "My friend Shalom is of an outstandingly kind nature and often helps those who seek him out. His only flaw is his addiction to good liquor. It is this very desperation for drink, however, that saves him from all other sins."[12]

This story illustrates a situation in which the soul communicates with the body through an addiction. Taking Shalom's liquor away from him would make him vulnerable to all other sins. Sometimes one cannot stop drinking or eating excessively without risking an even worse problem. It is as if one is saying, "I'd rather be fat," or "I'd rather be a drunkard." By doing so, one can be absolutely faithful to oneself, since losing weight or giving up an addiction could prove dangerous if the problem that would emerge—thanks to the decoding process, which transforms negative energies into fat or cellulite—is not taken care of beforehand. A diet must be more than a mere formula to eliminate symptoms; it must also uncover the deeper causes of the problem. In short, a good diet means self-knowledge.

Self-knowledge implies an examination of the intellect to identify the malfunctions in our decoding system. Once these malfunctions are recognized and the diet begins, the receiving flow is slowly restored and, gradually and almost imperceptibly, there is relief, recovery, and loss of weight. There is no shortcut back home. One's best choice is the direct route, which does not stray into byways—that is, regimens that aim exclusively at achieving an artificial body. Our body is the result of our emotional and spiritual history, of the choices we have made. To change this natural formation involves a gradual process; to change it recklessly can lead to imbalance or a denial of oneself. It might surprise many people to learn that their shape is what it is because that is what enables them to express themselves in the most authentic possible way. Exile is generally consolidated in the several different ways through which we wrongly try to open up our channels of receiving. A rush to the refrigerator in a desperate attempt to receive, for example, leads to serious consequences. "What keeps one in exile," the rabbis say, "is one's contentment at remaining in that situation."[13] And Reb Simḥa Bunam says that "the worst exile is the exile of learning how to live with it." In other words, people often say they want to be thin, but they don't really want it. They want to lose weight but are not interested in escaping their exile. They know what is behind their obesity and internally accept it, while externally making fruitless efforts to get rid of it. Instead of working to repair their receiving channels, they would rather follow a food-limiting regimen that simply reduces weight through some *technique*. The following story may illustrate this situation:

An acrobat once came to Krasny and announced that he would cross the river while balancing on a rope stretched from bank to bank. Rabbi Ḥayyim Krasner, a disciple of the Baal Shem Tov, was thrilled at the performance. Noticing his deep concentration, his friends asked him what exactly in the feat had caught his eye and made him so thoughtful.

The rabbi answered: "I was just thinking about the serenity with which the acrobat submits his life to such danger. You might say he does it for the coins that the crowd will throw to him. But that is not true, for if he thinks about that, he will surely fall right into the water. He must concentrate on one idea only: keeping his balance. He must prevent his body from leaning even a little bit to either side. His security depends on his determination to remain upright without thinking of any reward whatsoever. And that is the way human beings should cross their narrow rope of life."[14]

Although of course the acrobat hopes to earn a monetary reward for his feat, if for even an instant he deviates from his true task—that of concentrating on his balance and carrying out all the necessary micro-corrections in his movement—he will fall. Using a scale to measure our failure or success in receiving means not understanding that overweight is nothing but a side effect of bad receiving and of nonacceptance of one's body. Loss of weight would be merely a reward, and concentrating on it might mean that we lose our balance and fall into the water.

The fat/thin concept does not allow us to cross from bank to bank in a balanced way. We end up stumbling at every step on the rope. Still, we are sure to be in control if we worry about the water and the height rather than the steps we are taking. No scale but the inner one can tell us whether we are light or heavy. Sitra aḥra is what draws us away from a balanced step, by disguising itself as a scale and pointing to a way that is not a way.

The Evil Impulse

The worst exile is the exile from peace of mind. It is suffered by one who is overpowered by his evil desires at the same time that he is aware of their wickedness.

—The Belzer Rebbe[15]

"Evil" takes the form of impulses that are destructive to the lives of those around us and to ourselves. But does it make sense to speak of an impulse—meaning a will, a desire—as evil, as if it were not something we wanted? Do we want it or not? It would seem better to define an evil impulse as an ambivalent impulse or as a half impulse. So says the Maggid of Mezeritch:[16] "Study or any other activity in life that one does with only half a heart is of no use to either the body or the soul. He who lives half-heartedly is like someone who is half asleep."[17]

The sensation of division or ambivalence is what represents the sensory organ of the soul. In the same way that the nerves detect subtle changes in the body by monitoring our inner and outer exchanges, a "half heart," "quarter heart," and "whole heart" (*lev shalem*) allow for monitoring fluctuations of the soul. Suppose you want to be thin, yet you have an uncontrollable urge to rush to the refrigerator and stuff yourself, especially with food that is completely dissociated from your physical receiving flow because it represents either unnecessary or empty calories. Obviously this is not a whole-hearted situation! Such ambivalence is a sign that an evil impulse (*yetzer ha-ra*) is involved. The only way out is to recognize the ambivalence of your desire and launch a self-liberating process of redemption from your self-imposed state of exile. Reb Zalman Schachter-Shalomi once gave the following example:[18]

When a little baby is hungry, cold, lonely, frightened, or confused about what is going on around him or her, the mother offers her breast and feeds and comforts the baby. Then the child feels good once again. And what do we adults do when we feel hungry? We go to the fridge. When we are cold? Go to the fridge. When we're lonely? Go to the fridge. When we can't understand what is going on in the world? Go to the fridge. When we're depressed? Go to the fridge. When we want to get in touch with our essence? Go to the fridge. For the satisfaction of all these needs, it is appropriate for a baby to seek its mother's breast, which is the answer to all its problems. When we are grown up, however, we cannot expect all solutions to come through the same channel. And this spare tire here around our waist is a sign that we did not address the right source. In search of an instant solution to our problems, we turned to only one source when in fact we should have invoked many others.

It is a common problem to interpret different hungers—physical, emotional, mental, or spiritual—as only one kind: the hunger we feel at the refrigerator; and obesity is the physical outcome of turning these other kinds of hunger into physical hunger. Just as there are obesities resulting from physical malfunctions (which cause the body to receive mistaken information about how to manage its energy), there are obesities that represent a malfunction in the emotional, mental, or spiritual management of life energies.

But how can we tell when our eating is the wrong response to one of these other hungers? The "evil impulse," which I have called the half-impulse—a sense of inner conflict and a feeling of ambivalence, of not having one's whole heart in one's action—is often the major symptom. We should not disregard or suppress this symptom, but rather understand it. Indirectly at first, it can reveal significant ways of redirecting our hungers to their appropriate sources of fulfillment.

It's important to stress the complexity of this redirection process. Sometimes, for instance, emotional hunger may turn into physical hunger because a spiritual hunger has taken over the emotional space. It is not enough to try to convert hunger for food into hunger for sex, for example, without first redirecting one's hunger for power on the spiritual plane. The physical world cannot digest spiritual food, nor is spiritual food well absorbed through the mental digestive process. Thus we have to know ourselves in order to recognize when we are addressing the wrong food source for our hunger. Any ambiguity will translate into indigestion.

So what sort of discipline shall we follow in order

to direct our hungers appropriately? The Hasidic masters offer a short formula consisting of three different stages: (1) *kabbalah* (receiving), (2) *hakhna'ah* (subduing) and (3) *hamtakah* (sweetening).

1. *Kabbalah (receiving)*. In the first stage we allow ourselves to fully experience the rush to the refrigerator. Instead of fighting it, fully relish the impulse. Enjoy it all, from the sense of anticipation you feel upon opening the door sealed with its rubber gasket, revealing an infinity of options in the form of jams, cheeses, and pies . . . to the delicious sensation of control, which empowers you to pile up goodies on the kitchen table and to dream of creating daring taste combinations with an array of ingredients. As a microcosm of experience, the kitchen becomes the focal point in the house, a *kodesh ha-kodashim* (Holy of Holies). There lies the Holy Ark in refrigerator form—and inside it, the only chance for a connection to the future, to redemption itself. Let yourself feel it all, as if you were a High Priest marching toward holiness.

Inside this refrigerator-ark, however, there are no living foods but only static energy forms disconnected from the life process. All of a sudden, instead of serving God in a holy manner, one actually commits an act of *avodah zarah* (idolatry, literally, "strange service"). Such service to the god of escapism and materialism turns out to be an even deeper plunge into darkness— not a service but a disservice.

This is the very nature of yetzer ha-ra, the evil impulse: "Today it tells one, 'Do that!'; tomorrow it says, 'Now do this!'—until it ends up saying, 'Go worship idols!' and one just goes and does it."[19]

Allowing oneself to live intensely in the moment while under the influence of the evil impulse is a way of challenging it, since it usually comes disguised behind ambivalence or half-heartedness. One has to be on guard not to fight the impulse at the wrong moment. This is the stage when a wrong half-impulse holds sway over the situation. This is not the time to oppose, for instance, a physical hunger with emotional reasoning. It is the time to oppose the physical hunger with the emotional hunger that it displaced. Once this hunger is identified as not pertaining to the material world, the next stage arrives, that of hakhna'ah.

2. *Hakhna'ah (subduing)*. The idea of subduing this original impulse when the voice of our "good angel" tries to bar access to the refrigerator and pleads in a melodramatic tone, "No, don't do it!" seems repressive and forced. The problem is that we are under the power of compulsion whether we are irresistibly drawn to the refrigerator or forcing ourselves to move away from it. The seemingly external voice of conscience appears to be the only force capable of repressing our true inner essence. But what is this "external" force? It is certainly not the body, soul, or intellect. It is the displaced desire or need that we are mistaking for hunger.

And that is what our pathetic inner voice tries to do. It says, "You don't want that, you just think you do!" In fact, the problem our conscience faces is trying to counter the power of pies and pastries with abstract ideas. We ask our conscience, "Are you saying that in the middle of this chaos of internal voices, I'm supposed to figure out which one is the real 'I'?"

"Mm-hmm," replies the voice in the same emphatic, moralistic tone. But don't be prejudiced against its manner of speaking and acting; learn how to listen to its "Mm-hmm" in a new way.

We should not ask who the real "I" is in this internal consultation. Rabbi Yehiel Mikhel[20] once said: " 'I' is a word that only makes sense when articulated by God," the supernal source of life. At the same time, we have to give some credit to our inner voices and realize that they are not strangers to us. After all, they have a lot more in common with us than a slice of pie in the refrigerator does. So although it's wise to be skeptical about "hearing voices," let us realize that we are the one who is actively producing them.

Each voice has something important to tell us. One voice is screaming that you are hungry and must be fed. We must listen to this, because if we don't acknowledge the hunger, there will be no end to dieting and worrying about our weight. The other is yelling "Stop!"—and it, too, has a point: "Yes, you're hungry, but please, don't eat, because your hunger is not for food. Wake up and 'eat' what you really need!" It tells us that for the sake of our health, happiness, and fitness, it is worth facing the discomfort of dealing with the real source of our compulsive eating.

These are voices neither of the past (the repressive and moralistic tone of our conscience) nor of the future (the anticipated reward of filling our stomachs and whatever else is empty in other worlds). They are voices of the present, the only arena where it is possible to respond to this challenge in the name of "I." The present is the instant when the acrobat takes a step, when the step is all there is. There is the shore that we leave behind and the one that we step toward. But it is precisely at the moment of this step that we can contact the truth. Freeze the image of the hand pulling at the refrigerator door handle and ponder the words of Rabbi Isaac:[21]

> What was Adam's true sin? His true sin was worrying about tomorrow. The serpent deluded him when saying, "You are an unqualified servant, incapable of telling good from evil. Eat from this fruit and you will become a useful servant, knowing how to choose the good and being rewarded for that." And Adam, worried about the future, heard this and ate the fruit. If he had concentrated on his responsibility in that moment—

which was not to decide between future good and evil while in the presence of the serpent—he would not have done that.[22]

The serpent makes us worry about the future: it whispers to us about losing so many pounds per week and prevents us from recognizing the actual significance of diet. It takes a few weeks to notice the effects of a food-limiting regimen, whereas the results of a diet are noticed in the very first instant. This is so because when we are engaged in a diet, we feel lighter with a sense of renewal and health that is felt from its very beginning. And in that first instant we are also beset by the inner voices trying to trick us. To unmask them is to both subjugate and discredit them, as the following story shows.

A man decided to put himself to the test: he would spend Saturday without drinking or eating. As the day neared its end, an irresistible thirst came over him and he went straight to a well. But just as he was about to quench his thirst, he managed to control himself. He felt terribly unhappy, however, because he noticed that what had made him restrain his impulse was his pride in his ability to do so. There he remained— between wanting to drink and being too proud to drink—close to despair, until finally he noticed that his thirst was gone.

The next day, he looked for the rabbi of his village to find out what had happened and how he should have behaved. The rabbi explained: "There are two types of souls: the whole ones and the patchwork ones. Yours is the second type."[23]

When we perceive the voices as external forces compelling us to do this or that, we are like a patchwork. That is why we must intensely experience our impulse to go to the fridge as an internal impulse. External reasoning cannot counteract the strong desire that draws us to the fridge—it is merely one god opposing another. In a true diet, as contrasted with a regimen, the ultimate goal is to guard against idolatry—that is, to resist running after what is not absolute and losing touch with our deepest and most authentic self.

Hakhna'ah (subduing), in this sense, is not sublimation—exchanging one god for another. It means finding one God Who is behind the most trustworthy and consistent voice that arises within us. Hear it with all your heart (*Shema . . . bekhol levavekhah*), and not half-heartedly.

3. *Hamtakah (sweetening)*. Having understood some of the hidden symbolism behind our food addiction, we will find that the third stage comes in handy— that of "sweetening," or transforming the initial impulse without resorting to violent or traumatic mea-

sures. It must be a true transformation and not just a simple displacement, which would end up fattening us in other worlds. Reaching for the fridge is like worshiping before a false holy ark, which prevents us from understanding the nature of our problems and our obesities.

It was this very displacement that was at the heart of our earlier story about Shalom and his liquor. In a case like his, the internal voice urging a visit to the refrigerator is not evil. On the contrary, it is the best impulse that can arise in exile. One has to follow one's intuition. After all, no one understands exile better than the one who is in exile. But all those who are looking for change and who dream of shortening the journey home should work to transform themselves.

To work on ourselves requires a measure of self-knowledge. How do we acquire this knowledge? Through self-observation. We must pay conscious attention to what we do. Catching ourselves raiding the fridge can therefore teach us a great deal. Transformation can only take place if we are able to "sweeten" without losing contact with our will to both save ourselves from the clutches of the fridge and take responsibility for our health and fitness. To achieve that, we need a broader and more holistic commitment to who we are and what we stand for.

Sweetening is the most complex part of the formula, for it has to do with understanding the origin of our particular hunger, our need to receive, and why we ended up displacing it onto eating. In reality it seems like a strange thing to do: If we are so hungry for one thing, why would we go looking for something else? How can our desire be so important and urgent and at the same time be forgotten and ignored?

The Hebrew-language poet Ḥayyim Naḥman Bialik once wrote to a very dear friend: "Since I don't know what to tell you, I'll write you this long letter." Apparently, when we are emotionally involved, it's easier to write a long, roundabout letter than one that's short and to the point. We all write "long letters" that take us to the refrigerator or some other "address" because we have trouble dealing with real "home issues," and many times we simply do not know how to express our urges. The true answer might be hidden in the very suggestion of making it "sweet"—in Hebrew *matok* (M-T-K)—for when we apply the kabbalistic technique of reversing the root letters to find out what more we can learn about the meaning of a word, this word turns into *takum* (T-K-M), or "Rise!" To sweeten means to be able to lift out of our unconscious the deepest needs that have remained unexpressed, or expressed only through very long and unclear letters.

We have all experienced at least some moments when our good sense prevails and we forgo a desired food because it might be harmful to our health. When we do that, we are broadening the scope of our interest so as to perceive needs other than the most immediate ones. This is done in a friendly way because it is as if we are "convinced" from within that this is what is best for us. Integrating and harmonizing our voices, instead of seeing them as warring external forces, is what is called sweetening. From that perspective, our fridge experience is an important opportunity for growth. When we come to terms with our urges, guilt feelings, and expectations, we are making things sweeter.

When it comes to food, *sweetening* is a highly loaded word. We don't usually associate sweets with fighting fat. But here we are speaking of the process of reassigning hungers to their appropriate worlds by sweetening our feelings. Every time we can make peace with our inner conflicts, we create a sweetness that makes us lighter instead of heavier. Painful though it might be, self-knowledge always ends up in sweetness, not in bitterness. Those who restrain themselves on a true diet do not suffer as in a food-restricting regimen. Regimens are aimed at banishing strange hungers and require us to be constantly on guard lest they return. A diet, representing a connection to life itself, always involves some personal growth or transformation, for it means learning to sweeten our conflicts.

Overcoming Bad Habits

The Liadier Rabbi once said: "I devoted twenty-one years to finding my truth. It took me seven years to learn what truth is, seven years to get rid of falsehood, and seven more years to acquire the habit of sincerity."[24]

The Liadier here describes the process of shattering habits by moving from suffering to insight, from intention to action, and eventually from habitual behavior to personal transformation. Getting to know one's truth implies seven effort-years to acquire insight and self-knowledge. Seven more years are needed for getting rid of the falsehood produced by living out one's illusions. It takes another seven years to integrate these learning processes as an essential part of who one is.

In order to accomplish the last seven-year stage, one has to devote oneself to making subtle changes in attitude and behavior, when dealing either with others or with oneself. Such imperceptible changes mature from changes in attitude into changes in one's very being, as the following story suggests.

> A certain villager lamented to the Rebbe of Kobrin that his evil desires constantly overcame him and caused him to fall into transgression.
> "Can you ride a horse?" the rabbi inquired.
> "Yes," answered the man.

"What do you do if you happen to fall off?"

"I get on again!" asserted the man.

"Well, imagine the evil impulse to be the horse," concluded the rabbi. "If you fall, get back on, and eventually you will master it!"[25]

The diet I have been defining in this book is a lifetime effort in which the central virtues are perseverance and patience. Many give up such effort, complaining that it requires too much sacrifice; they feel it is better to grow fat and give up a little of their good health in exchange for enjoying life more intensely. They fail to realize the difference between a diet and a food-limiting regimen. A diet is in no way a sacrifice; on the contrary, it should generate a sense of pleasure. A sense of well-being is achieved not only through the effects of healthful practices but through the very act of taking good care of ourselves. Regimens, by contrast, are nothing but aimless effort and sacrifice, whereas diets mean a new way of life. Diets imply constant change, being constantly on the move.

Changing has to do with being able to free ourselves from conventional attitudes that we repeatedly imitate without realizing it. The more they are repeated, the more vulnerable to the evil impulse we are. And this tendency to form habits—which are something mechanical that is neither thought about nor chosen—ends up blocking us from freeing ourselves. A story about the lighting of candles on the Sabbath exemplifies this fact. Legend has it that when returning home from work or the synagogue on the Sabbath eve, a person is escorted by two angels, one on either side, a bad one and a good one. On arrival, if he finds that the Sabbath candles have been lit, the bad angel will have to humble itself and say along with the good angel, "So be it next Sabbath!" If, however, the candles have not been lit, it will be the good angel who is forced to utter along with the bad one, "So be it next Sabbath!"

Every time attitudes are put into action, they reinforce themselves. As depicted in the story, there is no impartiality—we either change or become more the same. Rabbi Aaron of Karlin used to say, "Those who do not rise, fall; those who do not get better, get worse." One who follows a regimen is like one who follows a recipe without paying attention to what he or she is doing, or taking medicine while repeating again and again the unhealthy behavior that caused the illness to begin with. The one who avoids dealing with real causes and real hungers is sure to suffer a relapse. At every relapse, one gets farther and farther from the goal, for attitudes are never neutral. Relapses reinforce our habits even more, to such an extent that the regimen becomes just another one of our habits.

Consider the following story, in which someone

complains about not being able to care for his health
without the help of a regimen or the constant presence
of a nutritionist:

> A young rabbi unburdened himself to his master:
> "While I am studying I am filled with light and
> life. But as soon as I stop, my feelings go away.
> What should I do?"
>
> The Rabbi answered: "You are just like the
> man who wanders in a forest in the middle of a
> dark night. He is accompanied halfway by a per-
> son carrying a torch. But there comes a time when
> their paths diverge and he must carry on alone. If
> he had his own light, he would not fear dark-
> ness."[26]

A regimen can never provide us with our own
light. A diet, however, is the internalization of our real
needs, allowing us to be constantly in touch with life
and the channels of receiving. Dieting gives us our own
light to illuminate a healthy path. Following regimens
just multiplies and compounds our difficulties, leading
to a loss of self-esteem. We often fail to grasp the importance of the present moment as the raw material from
which we can mold what we will become. Every single
present moment is the only thing that matters, not one's
past or future. It is in this instant that we should ask
ourselves, in the famous words of Rabbi Hillel:

If I am not for myself, who will be for me?
And if I am for myself only, what am I?
And if not now, then when?[27]

A good diet is made possible when it begins with a realization of our potential for life at any given moment. Any moment is a "now that can ignite the process of care and concern for ourselves and our fellow human beings. When we take responsibility for our life, we reconnect with its flow and begin to reverse any process of obesity.

Rabbi Shlomo[28] used to ask: "What is the worst thing the evil impulse can achieve?" And he gave the answer: "It can make you forget your own grandeur, having been made in the Creator's image and likeness."[29]

Anytime we disparage ourselves, we misread our potential and settle for less than we really are. The more we repeat this behavior, the more we lose the right to fulfill our own potential. You might think that settling for less, *being* less, would lead you away from obesity. In fact, this is one of the major reasons why people become attached to food, or to anything else that seems possible to control or grasp within the limits of the small "I." The "I" can become so small that there is nowhere to go but fatter.

3

THE HOLISM OF
THE RABBIS

Asiyyah: The World of Action

Blessings: Awareness of Substantiation

> . . . Keeping one's digestive system working per-
> fectly is as hard as splitting the waters of the Red
> Sea.
>
> —*Avot de Rabbi Natan*

It is hard to accept that food becomes part of us when
we swallow it—that we are what we eat. Just as the
biggest obstacle to ecological awareness is ignorance of
the consequence of one's actions, so it is with nutritional unawareness. When we forget that we are not a
garbage pail, a good part of the food we ingest is mal-
absorbed, thus creating an immediate and cumulative
toxicity.

Just by paying attention, we can learn a lot about our everyday nutrition. To eat with awareness means operating simultaneously on a theoretical level (where our understanding and discernment are based on cultural and scientific factors) and on a practical level (which depends on sensitivity to our own body). These two kinds of awareness are developed as a result of discipline and training. One has to find a cultural way to restore the instinct lost as a consequence of the acquisition of culture.

Jewish tradition offers a handy tool specially designed to substitute for the repressed instinct in human beings, making us aware of our food intake. This system is called *berakhah*, literally "blessing," which is essential in Jewish attitudes toward food. Blessings over food generally carry a devotional sense of thanksgiving, and Judaism also has this kind of blessing—but it comes after the meal, unlike in other traditions, where grace is said before eating. Another understanding, however, views the act of blessing as actually having a transformative effect on the food. The Ari explains:

> My master taught me that the first step toward the *ruaḥ ha-kodesh*, the Holy Spirit, is the blessing over food. Kelippot attached to food, and to people as a consequence, are thus drawn away. When you recite the blessing with intention,

harmful husks are removed, thus purifying the bodies ingesting them. That way food becomes spiritually neutral and transparent, ready to perform its tasks. My master very much stressed that aspect.[30]

Blessings over food give us the opportunity to pause before every act of ingestion and become aware of both the action we are about to engage in and the kind of energy we are about to take in. The blessings come in various forms, related to the energetic source of food. These include:

1. Food that grows in the ground: "Blessed art Thou, our God, King of the Universe, Who creates the fruit of the earth" (*peri ha-adamah*).

2. Food that grows on trees: "Blessed art Thou, our God, King of the Universe, Who creates the fruit of trees" (*peri ha-etz*).

3. Baked goods, such as cakes and pastry: "Blessed art Thou, our God, King of the Universe, Who creates various kinds of food" (*minei mezonot*). This does not include bread, the most basic of foods, which has its own blessing (next page).

Food is thus mentally associated with its original energy before every act of ingestion. Another two blessings are of a different nature and cover specific cases:

4. Foods transformed by natural fermentation.

   WINE: "Blessed art Thou, our God, King of the Universe, Who creates the fruit of the vine" (*peri ha-gafen*). Wine was special because it was the only known substance through which altered states of consciousness were achieved in the ancient Middle East.

   BREAD: "Blessed art Thou, our God, King of the Universe, Who brings forth bread from the earth" (*hamotzi lehem min ha-aretz*). Bread is the primeval food resulting from fermentation, a magical transformation.

5. Foods not regularly eaten, foods never tasted before, or the first foods of the season: "Blessed art Thou, our God, King of the Universe, Who has kept us alive, sustained us, and brought us to this season." This blessing, known as the Sheheheyanu, is also used at other moments when we take in an energy, situation, or emotion with this quality.

The berakhah is an automatic brake on the impulse of eating without awareness of the act or the energies it involves. When trying to free ourselves from the mechanical addiction of grabbing food and stuffing it into our mouth, we can say these blessings over our food and thus form good habits that will help us to resist bad habits.

A Hasidic allegory is told:

A man, who had gotten rid of bad habits under the supervision of Rabbi Lekivitzer, complained that he was often attracted to his old bad habits. The rabbi answered:

"I know of a tavernkeeper who constantly suffered from the violence and havoc wreaked by his customers. Because of this he converted his tavern into a quiet greengrocer's shop. One day a drunkard who was used to stopping by the tavern for a drink knocked at the door and asked to come in. Was the owner shocked by this? No—he understood that it was only natural for an addicted man under the influence of alcohol to forget that the shop had undergone a radical transformation. All he had to do was remind the man that his business had changed, and he instantly went away.

"The same thing happens to you. It is only natural that you yearn for your old habits. But just remind yourself that your life is completely altered now, and your desires will immediately leave you!"[31]

The berakhah is the inner tavernkeeper whom each of us must cultivate. Before eating anything at all, we must know who he is. Only after we get to know the nature of his business can we behave accordingly. Getting to know what one is before ingesting anything might seem slightly complicated. That is exactly, however, what happens to all other animals. We human beings need blessings to raise our consciousness of who we are in relation to food energies.

Kashrut: Awareness of the Energetic Essence of Food

Since the destruction of the Temple, every table in every house has become an altar.

—*Pesahim 4b*

Diet in the observance of Jewish tradition is governed by a set of laws called *kashrut*, literally "that which is appropriate." Kashrut is based on laws found in the Bible, which have been elaborated upon by the rabbis since before the beginning of the Common Era. This system has the function not only of developing self-control but also of transforming the individual. It is written in the Bible regarding these laws: "For I am God, your Lord, and since I am holy, you must make yourselves holy and remain sanctified" (Leviticus 11:44) and "You shall be holy to Me, for I, God, am holy" (Leviticus 20:26). The laws concerning the purity of food are thus aimed at sanctifying the individual and ultimately at preserving life itself.

When God offered the Torah to the Jewish people, according to legend, they first said, "We will do [obey]" (Exodus 19:8), and then added, "We will listen." At that point, the Talmud says, a Voice from the Heavens spoke: "Who disclosed that secret to My people?" [32] What secret was the Voice referring to? To the fact that our actions influence our way of thinking and being— that performance of the commandments leads to belief and discernment. In other words, you are what you do. The laws of kashrut encourage us to act in a way that affirms life. Food is considered proper or adequate according to whether or not it promotes life.

In brief, these laws consider all fruits and vegetables kosher (*kasher*, appropriate). All fishes with scales and fins and most domestic fowl are kosher. Nonscaly fishes, crustacea, and wild fowl are forbidden. Among mammals, only those with cloven hooves and that chew their cud are permitted. Following that criterion, a pig, which does have cloven hooves but does not chew the cud, is forbidden, whereas the cow, which fulfills both requirements, is allowed. Permitted fowl and mammals must undergo a ritual slaughtering process in order to be considered kosher. This procedure requires special techniques of blood draining and has to ensure that the animals do not suffer during the slaughter.

The strict limitations imposed by kashrut promote discipline and self-awareness. Different foods are either compatible or not, depending on which of the following categories they belong to: (1) *fleishig*, based on meat, (2) *milchig*, based on milk, and (3) *parve*, which is neutral. Fish, fruit, and vegetables are parve. Therefore they may be eaten together and with other foods. Meat and fowl are fleishig and cannot be combined with dairy products. After eating meat products, one waits three to six hours before taking any dairy products. The law forbidding the mixing of meat and milk is derived from a biblical command, apparently motivated by respect and compassion toward animals: "Do not cook a kid in its mother's milk" (Exodus 23:19). This principle of respect for life also rules the habit of draining the blood from kosher meat. Eating blood is forbidden: ". . . for the life force of the flesh is in the blood" (Leviticus 17:11).

This reverence for life is thus expressed in the daily diet, both when separating meat from milk (kashrut and when ritually slaughtering animals (*shehitah*). When eating means killing other living beings, a dietary system is just not enough. An attitude of assuming responsibility for one's food, before God or Life, is imperative.

A diet that promotes the life principle is crucial, for it broadens the notion of diet. A diet is an ecological and organic way of reconnecting with the life flow and health. This implies a physical fitness consonant with one's build, age, and ecosystem, which ultimately translates into a positive attitude toward life.

People often think that they cannot be attractive and lovable unless they work out or eliminate cellulite or fat deposits on the body. Actually, what is really attractive about a man or woman has a lot to do with the health of that person's connection to life. A lack of harmony with life produces an impurity that acts to separate people from those whom they want to be close to. They can come to envy the entire world from afar, without understanding why it is not theirs. The reason they cannot benefit from life is that they drive themselves away from the life flow of energy and exchange.

Kashrut redefines overweight in terms of a lack of awareness of the true flow of life. Any diet aiming at reordering just part of the receiving cycle not only is ineffective but also complicates even more the problems that make one resort to the diet. It ceases being a diet then. Kashrut implies the inspection of every food, determining whether or not it strengthens and affirms the life principle. It assumes a new concept: *Leḥayyim!* "To life!" (the words of a traditional Jewish toast). The best diet is one based on holistic principles, tailored to the individual.

The mind may question the logic behind the prohibition of mixing fleishig and milchig products as an effort to conform to a life-affirming diet. Experience, however, teaches that engaging in a conscious discipline can reveal new ways of connecting with life. What might at first seem like an archaic concept ends up creating a subliminal intention that becomes internalized and slowly transforms the way we relate to the world around us.

The incompatibility of meat and dairy has made observant Jews develop the habit of carefully studying the labels and chemical ingredients of any products to be eaten or otherwise or introduced into one's organism. Making the effort to determine whether a food is milchig, fleishig, or parve leads one to becoming acutely aware of the foods ingested. According to a careful classification system, several chemical products are either forbidden or not recommended—various sweeteners (glycerin, glycine), preservatives (stearate, stearic acid, argol), emulsifiers (mono- and diglycerides, polysorbates, magnesium stearate), enzymes (pepsins), acidulants, conditioners, aromatizers, stabilizers, antioxidants, and softeners—for most of these compounds derive from animals that were not subject to ritual slaughter.

These products might not be forbidden by biblical or rabbinical edict, but their chemical complexity imperils their kashrut. The rabbis who study these matters publish lists informing readers about the chemical ingredients in most common products on the market.

It is true that these prohibitions are merely concerned with (1) the methods by which animals are to be ritually slaughtered, (2) the possible combination of meat and dairy products, and (3) the dubious status of the origin of such products. The individual's awareness of ingesting only kosher foods, however, has to be directly connected with the effort to promote life and has to constantly adapt to the most up-to-date awareness of what constitutes a constructive attitude towards that goal. Following a static kosher diet is therefore not enough. Based on kashrut, one must define a positive attitude toward life that takes into consideration his or her geographical, social, psychic, and spiritual environment.

Many contemporary rabbis have pleaded for a minor redefinition of kashrut to include the prohibition of carcinogenic and contaminated substances. Reb Zalman Schachter-Shalomi suggests a kashrut that would include the awareness of electricity used in the home. He wonders: Does such energy come from a nuclear reactor that endangers life on this planet? Where does this light come from? Will it be to life (le-ḥayyim)? If it is not, then it is not appropriate (kosher). There are rabbis who consider aerosol sprays nonkosher, or against life, due to their power to destroy the ozone layer surrounding the planet. As radical and impracticable as these notions might appear, they are of much value once they improve our consciousness. They help us formulate a strategy, an agenda, in our relationship to life. By making use of energy derived from a source contrary to the principles in which one believes, one is receiving in the manner of the Dead Sea—without caring about how the flow will be passed on. In this way one gradually disconnects from the life chain and ceases to be attuned to the receiving process. Avodah zarah (idolatry) is the technical term for being out of touch with life.

In addition to making individual effort, it is important to look for a community whose vision of kashrut you share. Jewish tradition stresses the vital need to be bound to a group that adheres to similar "dietary" principles. Remember, we are speaking of diet in a broad sense, as the continual effort through which we are able to *receive*. Being part of a group engaged in the search for a broader consciousness of the network of interconnections that is life—whether ecological, political, or nutritional—offers essential support.

The preparation of food is another consideration of kashrut. We should not eat something if the manner of its preparation is doubtful or unknown to us. Over time, observing the religious prohibitions produces an instinctive attitude of attraction or aversion to particular foods. If you are uncertain about a food's preparation, take care before eating it. The place you stop for a snack should meet minimum requirements in regard to food preparation, and not just concerning hygiene. Even when eating a healthful or wholesome food, be attentive to the energy or atmosphere of the place. How is the food sold, brought to the table, and referred to by the people who prepared it? Is there a sense that it is respected and seen as the source of vitality and life for another being? What practices are followed regarding the use of utensils, specific tables for preparing specific foods, ventilation, refrigeration, or awareness on the part of the cooks or servers? The use of the same knives for several purposes; slicing machines used for slicing anything, from cheese to meats; grills being used to cook every type of food; and blenders mixing different liquids without being washed between blendings do not particularly indicate a lack of hygiene. What is lacking is the sense or respect and awe towards the sacred act of eating and feeding others. These details and aspects make us realize the meaning of a broad diet, which goes far beyond avoiding anything fattening.

A restaurant that sells food as an object or just another commodity is disconnected from the process of receiving. When eating at such a place, we, too, forget the nature of nourishment and take in energy as if we were absorbing an object. A nonreceiving cycle is thus established, which unfortunately ends in the body. As the least of the consequences, we are not ingesting living energy that transforms into our very being, but rather something that will end up just hanging there on our thighs or belly. A narrow diet leaves us full of lifeless "things." Cosmically speaking, we also become vessels that are closed to life and energy flow. As the principle of life fluidity, kashrut refuses to deal with energy sources as "things."

Yetzirah: The World of Formation

Ecological Awareness

Every diet, no matter how primitive, involves ecological principles that serve to ensure the survival of the species. Human culture has always preserved such instinctive principles. Hunters and shepherds have always moved from place to place so as to allow nature to recover from their activities in a certain locale until they return to it. Farmers became acquainted with the poten-

tiality of the land and knew that they should periodi-
cally allow it to lie fallow so as to rest and recover.

In the Jewish diet, such principles were preserved,
even though the situation of the people underwent some
transformation over time. As previously seen, food taboos might have originated in ancient principles of ecological preservation. The ecological care of the land is
clearly seen in the Sabbatical cycle (see Exodus
23:10–11), whereby a year of rest for agricultural land
was observed every seventh year in ancient Israel. Land
ownership was also restated on these occasions as an
extension of the receiving flow of life, of holiness, of
divinity, and not as emanating from an individual's
right to property. The fencing around the farmland was
removed and its produce no longer belonged to a single
owner.

The effect of these collective concerns on the individual is of particular interest here. When followed
from childhood, the discipline of eating according to the
seasonal availability of foods, along with the limitations
imposed by the group regarding the use of the land and
food taboos, leads us to a different notion of our bodies
and their limitations—limitations that are not necessarily real in a material or physical sense. Vegetarians,
natural-food enthusiasts, those who follow macrobiotics,
and others with particular dietary disciplines believe
that some foods just cannot be processed by the diges-

tive system. It does not mean that they cannot organically digest the food itself, but that emotionally, socially, and spiritually they just can't absorb certain products. Just as no one regards grass or wood as a desirable food with anything to offer the body, there are those who regard certain foods as failing to offer any possibility of transformation into their own bodies and energy.

This abstract notion of the body and its limitations is built on a broader and more holistic perception than that provided by the stomach. It turns into an instinct, a perceptual structure concerned not with any immediate gain or pleasure but with a chain of realities invisible to the untrained eye.

This second nature—developed through ethnic or cultural practices—does not require an obvious stamp of health or hygiene. The purposes behind the traditional rules of various groups are often not based on linear rationality. This being the case, there is no point asking why a certain food would jeopardize one's health, as if the general rules of a diet were concerned with physical health alone.

In Judaism, the aim of all *mitzvot* (commandments) is "to purify people" (*Genesis Rabbah* 44:1). The concepts of *tikkun ha-guf* (repairing the body) and *tikkun ha-nefesh* (repairing the soul) are helpful in understanding this. According to Maimonides, tikkun ha-guf has to do with the educational process through which we learn absolute rules that are most certainly not an end in themselves. Such rules are nothing but a step toward our full maturity. We learn, for example, such absolute values as peace and truth. In everyday life, however, we experience the possibility of either obeying or violating even the most absolute rules. When we overhear somebody insulting someone else, should we tell the offended party about it in order to defend and uphold truth, or not mention it in order to defend and uphold peace?

Learning the rules and absolute values is only a first step, which is worth nothing unless we see the "le-hayyim" principle as their true basis. Hence repairing, or balancing, the body has to do with understanding the absolute rules, in this case the ones particularly related to diet. Nevertheless, worrying about do's and don'ts and musts and mustn'ts means limiting ourselves to tik-kun ha-guf, a balancing act that resembles a mere regimen. Such balance simply cannot stand up to the demands of daily existence, and does not keep us from gaining weight or becoming heavier in the spiritual sense. In fact, we should use tikkun ha-guf as a starting point and then learn to depart from it. Only then will we be able to decide whether or not a given rule or restriction makes sense for most situations in life, where there is always more than one issue at stake.

A complementary step is then needed, tikkun ha-nefesh, which will stamp this educational process as successful. It presupposes independence from collective rules as the sole determinants of our attitudes; we should resort to them only as tools for thinking and decision making. The one who achieves the balancing of his or her soul is an artist who is closely in touch with life, its language, its signs, and its forces. Tikkun ha-guf merely points to the course along which the energy of life flows. It gives no direction, however, and one can be very much on the right course but in opposition to the flow. In other words, one can achieve tikkun ha-guf and still maintain a very negative attitude toward life. Tikkun ha-guf by itself assures one of absolutely nothing. It is the expression of a Dead Sea, brimming with chemical elements that do not interact and that are retained in a stagnant form.

Undoubtedly a major problem for both individuals and humanity at large is being stuck at the level of tikkun ha-guf, which causes people to have a very strict and inflexible perspective on life. Much of the radicalism and fundamentalism that we see around us is the consequence of being locked into the level of tikkun ha-guf. This level can make us stagnate, thus bringing on obesity. We might think that we are in consonance with our principles, and we may in fact well be. We might even think that we took the right course in relation to a specific issue, and we might well indeed have done so. The direction in which we choose to go, however, might be diametrically opposed to the flow of life. Using sacred concepts and conventions, one can still act in an idolatrous way.

Being restricted to tikkun ha-guf means being on a regimen only, going by the book, following commandments mechanically, and feeling more and more enslaved to these rules. Living and eating become a burden, an obsession, which in fact draws us further and further away from balance. For this regimen to become a diet and make some sense, it is also vital that its theoretical basis should align with our perceptions and commitments in other areas of life.

Vegetarianism

The beginning of ecological awareness entails a greater sensitivity toward other life forms. This awareness is especially built on our relationship with those living beings that we use as food. In ancient times, animals that were the main source of nutrition for particular communities became their totems or divinities. On the one hand, they were hunted and killed; on the other, revered as little gods. Actually these animals represented the possibility for life, a way of receiving divine energy. Biblical theology brought together all these sources of life energy and, through monotheism, affirmed the existence of only one origin for all life. It seems that the biblical ideal was vegetarian. A certain reading of the Scriptures allows for the interpretation of the slaughter of animals was a concession to human weakness—which, however, might be revoked later, thus allowing a return to vegetarianism. The prophet Isaiah foresaw an era when "the lion, like the ox, shall eat straw" (Isaiah 11:7).

Such a vision is corroborated by the Talmud:

> Adam was not permitted to eat meat, as it is written: "Behold, I have given you every seedbearing plant on the face of the earth. . . . For every beast of the field, every bird of the sky, and everything that walks on the land . . . all plants shall be food" [Genesis 1:29–30].[33]

Meat, however, was allowed after the Flood, for it was said: "Every moving thing that lives shall be to you as food" (Genesis 9:3).

This interpretation suggests that animal slaughter was first allowed only at this time, when apparently the vegetation covering the land was totally altered. In order to make meat fit for ingestion, it has been placed under more restrictions and requirements than other foods. Meat raises the issue of having to reconcile killing animals with the concept of food as an expression of life. To what extent do we as conscious eaters have to care about the entire food chain, as opposed to our own immediate needs only? Nature seems to answer this question for nonconscious beings by affirming that they need not be concerned. Ecological awareness, as a product of human consciousness, seems to point in a different direction. On that account, some rabbis have asserted the ideal of living without flesh foods. The Talmud states that one should avoid meat unless he or she especially longs for it.[34] Naḥmanides teaches the importance of "You shall become holy" and that even those who "long for meat" are to practice moderation in meat eating, even though explicit permission is given for it.

Those who do not abstain from meat should at least be conscious of the violence involved in the act of slaughter and should follow strict conduct aiming at causing the least possible suffering to the animal; in addition, they must not become detached from the fact that they are responsible for taking a life. That is why extremely strict laws concerning ritual animal slaughter (*shehitah*) have been elaborated, and the person who carries it out (*shohet*) is rigorously trained following traditional instructions, which require the recitation of blessings and a spiritual posture. This person has to be an adult and not a minor, and must be free of any physical or mental condition that might hinder this work.

The animal must be slaughtered in the least painful way possible in order for the meat to become kosher, or edible. Skill and techniques have been developed for this purpose. The kind of knife to be used and the method of sharpening it, which are specified in detail, have proved efficient for this purpose, even compared with the technologically advanced methods of nonkosher slaughter. The slaughter must be as quick as possible; a single strike that cuts the esophagus or gullet, trachea, jugular vein, and carotid arteries kills the animal instantly. The method, which quickly cuts off 70 to 90 percent of the blood supply to the brain, seems to minimize suffering. If the animal struggles or is slow in dying, its meat is considered inedible.

Soon after the animal's death, a detailed examination of the body is carried out to find out whether there is any physical defect or serious infirmity that might end up on someone's table. Internal lesions or certain cysts render the meat inedible.

Behind the laws of tikkun ha-guf, there are life principles that must be carried on, complemented, and even reconsidered. A story by the Israeli Nobel Prize winner S. Y. Agnon shows that tikkun ha-guf, and the laws themselves, are not enough to reckon with the complexity of life.

It was told to me by Rabbi Shmuel Arieh: In my youth I lived in the village of Koshilovitz, the

same Koshilovitz that gained world renown because the Baal Shem Tov was a shoḥet there before his greatness was revealed. I met a shoḥet
there, an old man over eighty. I asked him, "Did
you perhaps know someone who knew the Baal
Shem?" Said he, "I have never met a Jew who
saw the Baal Shem, but I have met a Gentile who
saw him. When I was a young man I used to lodge
with a Gentile farmer. Whenever I would pour
water on a stone before whetting my slaughtering
knife, the farmer's grandfather, an old man of
ninety or a hundred, would shake his head. I used
to think it was due to his age. One time I sensed
that he was doing it out of disapproval. I asked
him: 'Why do you shake your head while I work?'
Said he, 'You are not going about your task in a
nice way. Yisroelki, before he whetted his knife,
would dampen the stone with tears.' "³⁵

One cannot deny the fact that meat eating involves
an act of killing a sentient being. Such discernment is
basic if we are to come to terms with life, even if it
does not mean that we stop eating meat. Just the mere
consciousness of the reality of what we are doing makes
room for us to behave in a way that sanctifies life, even
though slaughter is involved. At the same time, in order
to be a vegetarian or to observe slaughtering rituals, one
has to be consistent. Only if we assume a general atti-

tude of nonviolence in life, which is really incompatible with slaughter, should we abstain from meat. We should not become vegetarians for compassionate reasons if we cannot extend that compassion to other areas of life. Therefore, abstention from meat is not an obligation or a commandment, but an ideal. It is not about being wrong, but rather about willing and striving to be right. It is not the minimal expectation of our conduct but one that takes into consideration how sophisticated and holy we can become.

> Once, when Rabbi Yehoshua Heschel was on his way to visit with his disciples, he came across a very steep slope. Without hesitating, the rabbi got out of his carriage and climbed it on foot.
>
> "Holy Rabbi," asked his attendant, "why on earth did you get out of the carriage and climb the hill on foot?"
>
> "Because I am afraid the horse will testify against me in the heavenly court, for not having pitied it and for having made it carry me all the way up this steep slope."
>
> "So what?" the attendant retorted. "Would you not win the case by arguing that a horse was made to serve human beings?"
>
> "Yes," replied the Rabbi, "I have no doubt whatsoever that I would win—but I'd still rather go uphill on foot than get involved in a lawsuit with a horse."[36]

So eating meat is not a crime for which one will be punished by the Tribunal of Life. To sustain ourselves with food is surely itself a demand of life. Nevertheless, when it's a matter of being able to use our own two feet to go uphill, the vegetarian is the one who does not want to face a lawsuit with a cow or a chicken, despite being able to win the case.

Another vital principle is "You shall not destroy," which derives from Deuteronomy 20:19–20:

> When you lay siege to a city and wage war against it a long time to capture it, you must not destroy its trees, wielding an ax against any food-producing tree. Do not cut down a tree in the field, unless it is being used by the men who confront you in the siege.
>
> However, if you know that a tree does not produce food, then until you have subjugated [the city], you may destroy [the tree] or cut off [what you need] to build siege machinery against the city waging war with you.

These verses serve as the basis for the rabbis' warning against wasting resources, which goes against the philosophy of kashrut (or le-ḥayyim). Health and self-preservation are directly linked to saving and managing constructive energy. This notion transcends the idea that an energetically healthy food is one that provides merely nutritional value in a balanced way to our organism. Health goes beyond the individual realm as well as the present moment. Eating healthily is eating in such a way that we feed the collective web of life with energy now and in the future. We must recycle by, for example, sowing as we harvest. Only those activities are nutritional that protect life and create a balance so that the banquet can be laid forever. Therefore, feeding on animal or plant species that are in danger of extinction is not a kosher procedure; to do so would make us heavier and fatten us, at least indirectly.

The rabbis state that not even abundant food is to be wasted. They condemn the "dishonoring" of food, which includes wasting it both on one's plate and in one's stomach. They are so concerned about waste that they even warn against small actions like passing a glass of water over a piece of bread, for one might spill the water and spoil the bread.[37]

This concept encompasses not only nutrition but all kinds of vital energy. In the talmudic tractate of *Shabbat* (67b) one is instructed to adjust oil lamps or candles so that they do not burn quickly, lest they lead to waste. On the brink of the twenty-first century, we might think that excessive use of gas or electricity has nothing to do with putting on a few extra pounds. But one thing is for sure: whoever does not know how to receive correctly accumulates fat on both tangible and not-so-tangible levels. Although these latter realms are less tangible, overweight there definitely makes us less charming and attractive to others and to the cosmos itself.

Beriah: The World of Creation

Political Awareness

> A disciple once asked a rabbi: "Why is the stork called *ḥasidah* [which is also the Hebrew word for 'devout']?"
>
> The rabbi replied: "Because it often feeds its brood and worries about it with great devotion."
>
> "Then why is its meat not considered kosher?" retorted the disciple.
>
> "Because it worries solely about its own!" answered the rabbi.[38]

This little story shows that a healthy food chain (or, ultimately, life chain) is much larger than an individual's stomach, or even the needs of an entire family. Also relevant here is another, almost revolutionary concept developed by the rabbis, *oshek*, which forbids the oppression or exploitation of consumers or workers. In a life-affirming system, any food produced or sold under such conditions is considered inedible. Since human labor is part of the food-production process until the moment the food reaches someone's mouth, any exploitation of workers introduces a contaminating element into the food chain. Sooner or later, food contaminated in this way will harm the consumer, not because of any physical quality but because of something more subtle.

For this reason we must be consistent in our lives, so that our actions (particularly eating) reflect our attitude toward life as a whole. This might sound somewhat utopian, or even radical; it is, however, in the small and daily acts that we learn how to undergo transformation. This should not turn into an obsessive attitude, but an attitude of care and respect toward Creation—an attitude that will ultimately lead us to "Love your neighbor, for he or she is really *you*."

This concept goes back to the times of the Holy Temple, when sacrifice was practiced. In that ritual, animal blood was poured onto the earth and never ingested, so that one would not assimilate the soul embodied in the blood. The idea that "you are what you eat" is crucial on both the physical and political planes. If we are indifferent toward the source of our food, this may result in our being actively supportive of a life chain that goes against our own values and interests. For example, when we eat products resulting from the exploitation of workers or consumers, the quality inherent in the way the food came to our plates gets digested into our own system. From eating these foods we will tend to grow even more indifferent to other life forms and the planet itself.

It may seem weird that we should have to think about all this in order to be at our proper weight. Nonetheless, important and healthy accomplishments in life come through the effort of awareness. Freedom, in reality, is not unlimited detachment but the awareness of alternatives and possibilities for choices. In fact, being free means constantly exercising the power of choice. If we don't exercise it, we end up losing it, for freedom is nothing other than a healthy interaction between controlling and letting go. This is also the process by which we get fat—by not exercising our real power of choice. Through frequent denial of our connection to the life force, we get out of balance, and this is the ultimate cause of obesity.

The rabbis even make a connection between this kind of freedom and beauty. The more we are able to exercise the power of choice, the more attractive we become. Surprising as it may sound, the more we care about life in the largest possible spectrum, the more fit, beautiful, and holy we became, and this is noticed by others.

Atzilut: The World of Emanation

Fasting

Fasting was previously referred to as a nutritional representation of Atzilut, the world of Emanation. It is crucial in any diet, as long as one understands its value. In Jewish tradition, fasting is the central ritual of the major holy day on the calendar, the Day of Atonement.

When properly followed, fasting represents the perfect merging of our physical and spiritual natures. Fasting means feeding on a nonmaterial food. It is not a passive abstinence from food, but an active feeding on nothing. Once understood, this distinction allows us to discern a regimen fast from a diet fast.

In a regimen fast, the body is the primary focus of concern, whereas a diet is concerned with the perfect integration of body, heart, mind, and spirit. A short allegory narrated by the Lekhivitzer Rabbi makes the distinction clear:

> A peasant was on his way home from the market one winter day. He stopped at an inn, tied his

horse to the post, and proceeded to enjoy himself merrily. In the meantime his poor horse stood outside in the deep snow, without food or drink, trembling from the cold.

"In the same way," said the Lekhivitzer, "there are men who fast often, thereby torturing their bodies, at the same time that their thoughts—which are an index of the true personality of men—turn to worldly affairs. These men are like the peasant and his horse."

The infliction of suffering on one's body has nothing to do with the fast proposed in the diet of the rabbis. A true fast "feeds" the body in its most subtle dimensions. This fasting is an act of the body and at the same time transcends the body, for it means going without the real exchange of substances with the world—just as the hungers of the emotional, intellectual, and spiritual level do without material exchanges.

In true fasting, "peasant" and "horse" are merged into one single entity. But in what context? Should they both be outside in the deep snow, or should they both be inside the inn, warm and full of good food? The right answer is they should both be inside enjoying the warmth and the treats. To eat and drink on the level of the spirit can be represented in the physical world only by the abstinence from food (the fast). Every time this incredible kind of nonmaterial "supper" is made possible, we can feed ourselves in a symbolic way. And that is the reason why those who truly fast are not hungry. The Rabbi of Lentz once said: "One may fast only when he is so immersed in piety that he feels no hunger. But one who suffers from the lack of food may not afflict his body, since God dwells therein."[40]

For God to dwell therein, one cannot be split into a horse in the cold and a peasant at the inn. God resides in a person who is a whole being. Fasting represents a connection with the food chain, not a break with it. In other words, fasting is a true option of the body and in no way an act of neglect.

Fasting thus allows for the recognition of a special kind of hunger that can only be satisfied by not eating. This discovery provides us with a new vision of life that is profoundly healing.

Ecology and its insights into the limits of consumption have made us perceive that not eating is a way of feeding ourselves and of strengthening the life chain. Nomadic tribes of the past extracted food from the earth only to the extent that it could be renewed. The ability to control one's greed made not eating an ultimate act of nutrition. When we learn how "not to eat"—without resorting to any concept of abstinence whatsoever, but as a way of making a return to life out of our awareness of its bounty toward us—we reach a special level in the art of giving and receiving.

Fasting forges a connection with the original Power that feeds the universe and makes us aware of the amazing network of food of which we are a part. Not eating is often a more efficient way than eating of sensitizing us to the several hungers that play their parts in this total reality.

Balance of the Body

Awareness of Body and Matter

In the morning prayers, as noted in chapter 1, we thank God for the functioning of our body and pray for the open and closed parts to remain as they are. The rabbinical tradition considers the boundaries of the body as defining a sacred space. As a parallel idea to the bodily boundaries, the *mezuzah*, a parchment containing biblical texts, housed in a small case, is placed on the right doorpost (and often the inner doorposts) of a Jewish home, and Jews kiss it when entering or leaving. It is an amulet that distinguishes between the holiness levels inside a house and outside in the street. At home,

one relaxes and engages in intense and deep relationships with people. What one brings to and from the
home deserves careful attention.

Another ritual object is the *tefillin* (or phylacter-
ies), consisting of two small leather boxes that, like the
mezuzah, contain parchments containing biblical texts.
During prayer one of the boxes is placed on the fore-
head between the eyes by means of leather straps, and
the other one is placed around the left arm, close to the
chest. These two mezuzah-like boxes, next to the brain
and heart, represent the gates through which feelings
and emotions become part of us. Our intellectual and
emotional readings of the world are taken through these
gates. The tefillin warn us that we should be very careful about what we allow into those gates. Any thought
and emotion that we let in becomes part of our makeup.
We should guard against becoming contaminated by our
own limitations and partial understanding of reality
when we draw conclusions or feel an emotion.

Similarly, whatever we eat cannot be ingested before passing through the guardianship of awareness of
what we are bringing into ourselves. It has to be appropriate—that is, edible and digestible—in all the different dimensions from which we feed ourselves.
According to Rabbi Akiva: "He who eats food that is
not appropriate to him transgresses three command-

ments: he disrespects himself, he disdains the food, and he makes a blessing in vain [by sanctifying something that is unfit and unhealthy]."[41]

When we eat, we are responsible not only for our own health, but also for sociopolitical concerns of waste and conservation and for the health of our connection to all living things. Keeping fit is understood as an obligation not just to oneself but also to the cosmos. As the first-century Jewish philosopher Philo once wrote: "The body is the soul's home. Should one not, then, take better care of one's house so that it does not fall apart?"[42]

Hillel,[43] in Roman times, says something similar that illustrates the importance of the body even more. He considers the body holy in its own right, not just as the dwelling for the soul. And so is it told about him:

Having finished one of his lessons, Hillel once walked his disciples halfway to their houses and then bade them farewell.

"Where are you going, master?" they asked him.

"To carry out a mitzvah [religious duty]," he replied.

"And what mitzvah might that be?" the disciples insisted.

"Bathing myself in the mikvah [ritual bath]," he answered.

"Is that a mitzvah?"

"If the person in charge of cleaning and polishing the emperor's statues at the entrances of circuses and theaters is paid for his work and even seen as commendable, then undoubtedly it is only right that I, who was created in God's image and likeness, should take care of my body."[44]

The most serious obstacle to learning to respect the body is our inability to realize its status as our greatest possession. Dealing in very concrete, materialistic terms may give us the proper perspective:

Rabbi Bunam went to the market to buy beans. The farmer was not happy with Reb Bunam's offer and asked him, "Could you try and do better than that?" This question captivated the rabbi. From that day on, he often persuaded his disciples to engage in self-examination solely by repeating that very appeal made at the market, in the same earnest intonation: "Could you try and do better than that?"[45]

To know how to evaluate is a wisdom difficult to acquire. To be in touch with the real law governing the supply and demand of our body, emotions, mind, and spirit (in order to offer and receive a fair price in our exchanges with the universe) is a very complex matter.

In order for the market of life to become ecological—
that is, for life to get the most out of any given situation—we should consider in every exchange the real
need we have in supplying and the real need we have
in demanding. The best price should take into consideration not only how much we want to receive but also
how much we want to give.

This being the case, such an ecological concept
can also be applied to economics. Jewish tradition
states that profit is welcome in any transaction, provided that both parties profit. That is also the basic
principle of cooperation in nature: whatever there is to
be offered initiates an endless chain of exchanges in
which some will be at the giving end and some at the
receiving end, a process that generates profit for all.

Therefore, finding honest profits is a religious and
ecological obligation. In such a transaction, none of the
parties involved hold more than their share, so that the
true law of supply and demand prevails. An attempt to
get more profit than a transaction allows leads to loss
and to a disruption of the ecosystem between what is
available and what is needed.

Reb Bunam came to master the understanding of
the crude reality of the market, the one we usually refer
to as a "jungle." He understood that the secret of life is
to find the maximum value of things, a value to be set
naturally by the laws of supply and demand. If we know
how much we need something, trusting that the other

party will know how much it "needs" to offer it, then we can always try to do "better than that." Reb Bunam asked his disciples to measure their spiritual efforts in terms of their need to grow and to perfect themselves. They should never offer less, for even if it looked as if they were getting a profit, it would really turn out to be a loss. "Could you try and do better than that?" in the "jungle" marketplace demands a sincerity and trust in the life chain that few people get to exercise.

If we could perceive our body in the light of this reality, we would establish a different relationship with all that concerns us—including nutrition, physical exercise, and stress, among other things.

How much is physical exercise really worth? How much is it worth to fast, in exchange for more time or any other reward? How much is the stress of trying to achieve something or get somewhere worth? Knowing how to give value to these exchanges with reality, understanding the priorities and costs in any of these transactions, puts us in touch with our own time (our life) and our own space (the body). And there is great delight to be derived when we come to terms with our lives and our bodies. Maimonides calls attention to this aspect in particular, through the use of a concrete example:

> If one took care of his body as well as he takes of the animal on which he rides, he could prevent

many sicknesses and problems. For one will
never find a person who overfeeds his animal; he
will feed it to its capacity. Nonetheless, this very
person can eat excessively, with no measure or
consideration whatsoever. People are often attentive to the movements and stresses on their animals, to ensure that they remain healthy and free
of infirmities. They do not pay the same attention
to their own bodies, though.[46]

Moderation in Food and Other Substances

If you find honey, eat only what you need; otherwise
you will gorge yourself and throw it up!

—*Proverbs 25:16*

From biblical times, it has been stated that moderation is the most simple and efficient way to maintain
health and fitness. The Koretzer Rabbi[47] used to say:
"Eating moderately is recommended, for that way lon-
gevity is lengthened. Animals and reptiles show that
those who eat less live longer."

The challenge of eating moderately requires us to
focus on two points. Maimonides describes the first one
in a chapter entitled "Preserving Youth": If you are
hungry or thirsty, just wait a little, for it might be a
deceptive hunger or a deceptive thirst. Giving the body

a chance to confirm its request, we encourage an efficient and sincere dialogue with our physical needs. We
can allow ourselves this pause without anxiety, for we
know that if the body's request is repeated, it will be
granted.

The second point is not to eat rapidly. When you
feel hungry, make a ritual of sitting down and, if possible, meditate on your food (this is what the rabbis call
a blessing). This moment is a sacred interval, as the
Baal Shem Tov explained. We should not regard time
spent eating or sleeping as lost time. Our soul rests during these intervals, which allow us to reinvigorate our
holy service with renewed enthusiasm.

If the problem of overeating persists, more direct
words are needed, as in Ben Sira's[48] advice:

> If you are seated at a table with abundant food,
> do not lick your lips and exclaim: "Mmmm, what
> a treat!" Do not grab whatever is in front of you,
> and do not go ahead of the others; judge their
> feelings based on your own, and always behave
> accordingly. . . .
>   Polite people are content with eating little,
> and this prevents their heavy breathing after
> going to bed. Whoever eats moderately rejoices
> in a healthful sleep, wakes up early, and feels
> reinvigorated. Sleeplessness, indigestion, and
> colic are the glutton's share.[49]

Only through inner maturity will we learn how to moderate our food intake and achieve balance in what we retain. Very simple things like taking care of the quality of our sleep or cultivating awareness of our hungers are small but meaningful steps toward viewing ourselves as being more than just someone who craves a certain food in a certain amount. Maimonides warns, in "Preserving Youth," that such wisdom is not easy to attain: The wisdom of how to consume is hidden from the masses.

Maimonides advises not to go food-shopping either when feeling hungry or when having no appetite. The hungry shopper will buy much more than he or she needs, while the one who is not hungry will buy too little. Moderation brings us closer to our real need. The same goes for eating, strange as it might sound: we should never eat when hungry. If we go to the table starving, we will gobble up a lot of food rapidly, which will not adequately meet our true need. It is also not proper and healthy, as Jewish mothers know quite well, to sit down at the table when one has no appetite because of having eaten irregularly. In this way of thinking, fast food is the worst habit we can have. Not only is it poor nutrition, but also the act of eating in the quickest possible way is harmful to our digestion and our stress level.

Moderation should be applied not only to quantity and speed, but also to intensity. Because health is the balance between what is open and what is closed, what is received and what is given away, anything harsh or extreme is harmful. All energies and powers must be of the right strength or frequency so as to allow for their absorption and influence in a healthy way. Medicinal drugs, for example, have contributed much to the art of well-being; but everything that does good does it only to a certain extent. There is no medicine that cannot also be a potential poison when taken in an overdose. Trying to recover balance and health by relying on sources outside the natural exchange of life energies (that is, diet, sleep, and the like) should only be a last resort.

Samuel Ben-Meir, known as the Rashbam, calls for moderation in other ingested substances: "Do not take medicines or drugs, for they require periodical doses, and your heart will beg for them. You will lose money. And even for medical reasons, do not take medicines if you can find something different to heal you."[50]

This can be taken also as a warning against foreign substances to which we have become particularly alert in modern life, such as dyes, carcinogens, pesticides, stabilizers, and hormones, among other chemical additives or contaminants. Nowadays one must also be concerned about the exposure of food to radiation.

The Kabbalah of Fitness

In my book *The Kabbalah of Money*,[51] I raised the question: Who is considered rich? I went on to describe the notion of prosperity as related to resources and treasures in the different worlds—physical, emotional, mental, and spiritual. No matter how much you may own in the material world, that does not mean you are really rich. The rabbis observe that the rich are those who delight in their share (that life reserves for them). This is a way of saying that we are rich when we are satisfied with our material, emotional, intellectual, and spiritual resources.

In the case of food, we might similarly ask: Who is considered not fat? And we may answer that the not fat are those who are light in all worlds. Several times in this book we have noted that beauty and health are not privileges of the physical world alone. There are people of ideal weight and a finely sculpted body whose emotional life is so obese and neglected that others soon realize how unattractive these people are.

The different worlds are so interconnected to each other that we can never be fit if we are careless or obese in any of the worlds. In fact, to maintain fitness in all worlds, working out is necessary. Do you feel that you are already stressed enough from the amount of time you spend at the health club? Realize that taking care of the body is but a small part of the necessary workout. Instead of being stressful, any move toward health should offer great satisfaction. If your workout oppresses you, it may be because you are doing it only for external reasons, to alter your appearance. But what kind of workout would address our health in all life dimensions—the four worlds mentioned in the Kabbalah?

The Kabbalists had a great insight when intuiting that the different worlds are utterly and holistically interconnected. In each and every one of them, the presence of the others is implicit. There will always be an emotional component in the spiritual world and vice versa, as there will be a mental component in the emotional world and vice versa. Table 2 is an exercise in analyzing the physical or concrete component present in the different worlds. It will help us to understand concrete areas in which we may supplement our health measures in a practical way, expressing the characteristics of each world.

Everyone works out daily. Even pressing the keyboard on a computer is a physical activity. The body, of course, needs a higher level of activity than that in order not to accumulate too much fat. The same goes for vegetative, emotional, mental, and spiritual activities. Everyone performs activities on all these planes, but

Table 2
WORKOUTS IN THE FOUR WORLDS

World	Level of Interpretation	Reality	Workout
Physical ASIYYAH Structural World	KATUV Physical text; parchment and ink	Vegetative	Sleep
ASIYYAH Functional World	PESHAT Literal	Animal body	Exercise
YETZIRAH World of Formation	REMEZ Allusive	Emotional	Sexual activity and sensuality
BERIAH World of Creation	DERASH Symbolic	Mental	Meditation
ATZILUT World of Emanation	SOD Secret	Spiritual	Prayer

not enough to ensure health. Just as we need supple-
mentary physical activities, we should realize that we
need extra workouts in the other areas of our lives too.

On the vegetative level, sleep represents the renewal of an energy that is cyclical, as in the process by
which plants cyclically alternate their intake of carbon
dixoide and output of oxygen. In the animal world, this
vegetative element manifests itself in the cyclical need
for alternating periods of waking and sleep. Without the
pause that sleep provides, we lose the ability to integrate the different planes of reality, and we experience
confusion. We have to make healthful sleep a constant
workout, for that will help us not to become overweight
in physical activities (workaholism), feelings (obses-
siveness), thoughts (pessimism), or faith (depression).

In the realm of feelings, working out refers to the
way we deal with our sexuality and sensuality. Any form
of friendship and affection establishes a sensual relationship. This sensuality is a desire for communion, for
the feeling of delight in intimacy with other people. It
is, however, through sexual relations that the most concrete physical component in the plane of feelings manifests itself. A healthy sexual life is essential if one is
not to get "fat." This kind of workout prevents obesities
of the physical (tension and aggressiveness), mental
(being moralistic), and spiritual (alienation) planes.

In the mental world of Beriah, we are dealing with

a dimension where "physical" activities become more symbolic and subjective. In the mental world, a "physical" workout takes the form of meditation. Meditation is the technique of emptying the mind of the residues of everyday thoughts and mentalities. Such residues have to be cleaned up so as prevent them from turning into interference or noise in our mental activities. Just as computers need periodic checking to find lost files or clusters that make them slow and inefficient, so does the mind have a similar need. Meditation, whichever school or technique one may practice, is an exercise of the mind to prevent fats and excesses on the plane of thoughts. If we do not meditate, we will experience obesities in the physical (stress), emotional (intolerance), and spiritual (fundamentalism) worlds.

In the spiritual Atzilut world, the physical component is prayer. As subtle and abstract as the act of prayer may be, it still has a component in the physical world. This being the case, the physical act of praying or of trying to connect with the universe functions as a workout, as a compensation for whatever deficiency there is in one's daily "spiritual activities." We all feel an urge to offer praise or pray at the setting of the sun, when a particular song is played on the radio, or when we allow ourselves to be touched by life. Nonetheless, just as the body that sits all day at the computer needs an aerobic workout, the soul needs more than just short-lived moments of transcendence in daily life. Those who do not turn to prayer of some kind, from any tradition, become spiritually unbalanced. And this imbalance generates obesities on the physical (attachment), emotional (egocentricity,) and mental (megalomania) planes.

Even though this technique of analyzing reality by breaking it down into different worlds may seem no more than a game, it helps us to have a deeper understanding of our own nature. This game can certainly grow more complex. Whereas the spiritual component in the physical world is prayer, the physical component in the spiritual world is philanthropy or concern for others. Whereas sexual intercourse is the emotional component on the physical plane, the physical component on the emotional plane is the act of holding someone's hand, embracing, or kissing.

Those who are in good shape can place themselves above the average performance expected for their "existential stage" on the charts that measure fitness in the physical, emotional, intellectual, and spiritual planes. Each one should be able to establish a fitness schedule so as to sleep so many hours, exercise to a certain extent, interact sexually in appropriate ways, meditate regularly, and pray at certain times. Whoever does not put any of these modalities into practice gets out of shape. However, the greatest loss undoubtedly lies in missing the deep pleasure that comes with being healthy in all the worlds.

4

THE TABLE IS LAID

Shulḥan arukh, or "laid table," is a rabbinical expression for any processes in life that spread out before us so that we may start banqueting. This expression became popularly known among Jews when a code of Jewish laws concerning all areas of everyday life was compiled in the sixteenth century under the title *Shulḥan Arukh*.

It literally intended to lay Jewish law on the table so that ordinary, not particularly educated people could have access to the banquet. The laid table is the naked truth in its most crude and objective form. It represents that particular instant when one experiences and assumes total responsibility for one's life. The laid table is also a way of addressing the idea of the present moment, which turns out to be the only banquet within our reach. Represented in this table is not only the chain of giving and receiving that allows for the incredible possibilities laid on the table, but also the responsibility for the continuity of this process. To perpetuate this laid table is the task of every generation, a task that is always at stake at every moment that we are seated at the banquet. The state of our health, physical fitness, and appearance is merely a picture frame that instantly depicts the dynamic of this flow of give and take in our own lives.

So why does Jewish tradition apply the title *Shulḥan Arukh*, "The Laid Table," to its body of laws? It is because of the importance of this moment of being in direct relation and exchange with the banquet. Once we are seated before the laid table, we must not take it lightly. There is a fundamental process of life taking place there, and full attention to it is required from the participants in the banquet.

Jewish masters and sages were often accused of madness because they concentrated on the banquet table while the banquet hall itself was being consumed in flames. They were misunderstood. They knew that their last and only chance for liberation lay in their present commitment to that laid table. Hence, they went on exploring what was on the table, item by item (a process of thorough and meticulous reasoning that is called *pilpul* in Hebrew), as a technique for connecting to a broader reality.

Understanding how to behave before the laid table is vital knowledge. But whether it is our lives or a meal that is laid before us, we should not torture ourselves for not knowing how to behave. In reality this is, at the same time, the most simple and the most complex task we will ever face. We may panic and feel like jumping onto the table and devouring everything in front of us, as if the only law ruling the interactions at that table were to get the most out of it by filling ourselves up: We would like to be "champions of receiving," able to take possession of everything, including our own bodies. The result, however, is that our panic does not subside; on the contrary, it gets worse. In this we cannot approach the table without losing contact with the laws of receiving and getting fat. Reb Naḥman described this panic as a situation in which we cannot go forward but dare not retreat—and so we lose our way.[52]

The appropriate attitude before the laid table of life is to be wholly present and conscious in the moment. One should not fear to make a *faux pas* at the table, for one is charged only with what one can (and therefore must) give to oneself and to the life chain. As incredible as it may sound, this chain neither belongs to nor possesses anyone. Everyone is part of the chain; everyone *is* the banquet. Reb Bunam said:

> Thus it is written in the Bible (Exodus 30:13) that one should donate half a shekel [the coin of Israel] to the priests, as atonement for our mistakes and as ransom for our souls. Why only half? Because the other half is God's, Who created human beings with the evil impulse.[53]

According to this commentary, we should never feel alone in taking responsibility for our actions—we are only responsible for half of it. God is always a partner with us, since our very nature was given to us by the Creator. This is said not with the intention of taking from our shoulders the responsibility for life but to keep us from bearing excessive guilt, which could paralyze us. We have to know that the table as well as the feast is ours. We should not hold back out of fear of partaking of the banquet of life, since there is so much laid out on the table and so many ways of getting to it. Understand that the banquet is the very reason that we have been invited to the party.

The story is told of Rabbi Sussia's dying words to his disciples: "I fear the Heavenly Court." The disciples were dismayed: How could such a holy man be afraid of the Final Judgment? He then explained: "I am not afraid I will be blamed for not having been Moses, for I am not Moses. Nor am I afraid of being asked why I was not Maimonides, for I am not Maimonides. What I fear being asked is: 'Sussia, why were you not Sussia?' "

The table is set for us; the banquet is ours. And we know this. But that is no reason for us to pounce on the table like a starving person. That is certainly why we get fat. The principle may be correct: The banquet is ours. The attitude, however, is wrong. We are not to swallow the banquet without savoring it; to the contrary, we are meant to enjoy every nuance of taste, mixing cold and hot, sweet and sour, mild and spicy. Only with this attitude can we partake of the real banquet of life, in which we constantly toast to life and for life: Le-ḥayyim!

Rules of Physical Well-Being

Taking the laid table, or shulḥan arukh, at a more tangible level, let us look at a chapter from the *Kitzur Shulḥan Arukh* entitled "Rules Concerning Physical Well-Being."[54] The *Kitzur* is an abridgment of the *Shulḥan Arukh* written by Rabbi Solomon Ganzfried (1804–1886).

This anthology of rabbinical advice is, in fact, a diet, one that incorporates the principles of eating, even the purely physical act, according to the perspective of life as a banquet.

Digestion

1. Since it is the will of the Almighty that man's body be kept healthy and strong, because it is impossible for a man to have any knowledge of his Creator when ill, it is therefore his duty to shun anything which may waste his body, and to strive to acquire habits that will help him to be-

come healthy. Thus it is written (Deuteronomy 4:15): "Take you, therefore, good heed of your souls."

2. The Creator, blessed be He, and blessed be His name, created man and gave him the natural warmth which is the essence of life, for, if the natural warmth of the body should be cooled off, life would cease. This warmth of the body is maintained by means of the food which the man consumes. Just as in the case of fire, if wood is not added to it, it will be extinguished, so it is with a man, if he would stop eating, the heat within him would cool off, and he would die. The food is first ground between the teeth and becomes mixed with juice and saliva. From there it goes down into the stomach where it is likewise ground and mixed with juices, the juice of the stomach and the juice of the gall, and is reduced to dregs, and it is boiled by means of the heat and the juice, and thus becomes digested. The limbs are nourished by the pure parts of the food, and this sustains the life of the man, and the impure substance which is unnecessary is pushed towards the outside. And concerning this process, we say in the benediction *Asher yatzar* (who formest), the following: *Umafli lassot* (and doest wonderfully), which means that the Holy One, blessed be He, has endowed the man with the

nature to select the good part of the food, and every limb selects for itself the nourishment that is suitable for it, and rejects the waste out of the body; for, if the waste should remain in the body, it would cause many diseases, God forbid. Therefore, the good health of the body depends upon the digestion of the food; if it is easily digested, the man is healthy and vigorous, but if the digestive system does not function properly, the man becomes weak, and this may cause a dangerous state of health, God forbid.

3. Food can be easily digested when it is not too much and it is the easily digested kind. When a person eats too much and his stomach is full, the digestion is difficult for the reason that the stomach cannot expand and contract properly and grind the food as necessary; just as in the case with fire, if too much wood is placed on it, it will not burn well; so it is the case with the food in the stomach. Therefore, the person who wishes to preserve his physical well-being must take care to adopt the happy mean, eating neither too little nor too much, all depending upon the nature of his body. Most of the maladies which plague man arise either from eating unwholesome food, or from the excessive eating, even of wholesome food. To this, Solomon wisely alludes (Proverbs 21:23): "Whosoever keepeth his mouth and his

tongue, keepeth his life from trouble"; this refers to the person who keeps his mouth from eating unwholesome food and from gluttony, and keeps his tongue from speaking, except what is necessary for his daily needs. A certain sage said: "He who eats little from unwholesome food is not harmed as much as the one who eats excessively from wholesome food."

4. When a person is young, his digestive system is strong; therefore, he is in greater need of regular meals than the middle-aged person. The aged man, because of his weakness, requires light food, little in quantity and rich in quality to sustain his strength.

5. On hot days, the digestive system is weak on account of the heat; therefore less food should be consumed than on cool days. Medical scientists have suggested that in the summer, a person should eat only two-thirds of what he eats in the winter.

6. It is a known rule in medical science that before eating, a man should have some exercise, by walking or by working until his body becomes warm, and thereafter eat. And concerning this it is written (Genesis 3:19): "With the sweat of thy face thou shalt eat bread." And again (Proverbs 31:27): "And the bread of idleness she doeth not

eat." A person should loosen his belt before eating (those fond of *nutarikin*[55] find reference to it in the verse [Genesis 18:5]: "*Va-ekḥah pat leḥem*" ["and I will take a piece of bread"]. The letters of *ekḥah* [I will take] read backward are the initials of *Hater ḥagorah kodem akhilah* [loosen the belt before eating]. And the letters of *pat leḥem* [piece of bread] are the initials of the words *pen tavo leyedei ḥoli me'ayim* [lest you contract a pain in the innards]); and while he is eating, he should be seated or recline on his left side; and after the meal, he should not move about too much, so that the food may not reach the stomach before it is well conditioned and cause him harm. He should walk a little and then rest; but he should not take a long walk or tire himself out too much after the meal; neither should he take a nap immediately after the meal, before the expiration of at least two hours, so that the gases may not penetrate the brain and cause him injury. Immediately after a meal, it is not good to bathe, let blood, or have sexual intercourse.

Cold versus Hot Foods

7. Men differ with respect to their temperaments; some are hot-tempered, some cold, and others medium. Foods also differ with respect to applying bodily heat, and one whose temperament is

medium should eat food which is medium. But one whose temperament is not medium should eat food which is a trifle reverse to his temperament. One whose temperament is hot should not eat hot foods, such as spices and balsam plants, but food which is cool and somewhat fermented; and one whose temperament is cool should eat food which is a little warm. The food should likewise be prepared according to the season of the year and the place; in the summer, one should eat cool foods, for instance, the meat of tender lambs and goats and spring chicken, and also a little of fermented foods; but in the winter, one should eat food that generates heat. In a cold climate one should also eat hot food, but in a warm climate, cool food.

Wholesome Foods

8. The medium food is wheat bread, but not the kind made out of pure fine flour, because fine flour takes long to digest; but it should contain some of the bran, moderately leavened and salted, and baked in an oven; the other kinds of food made out of wheat are not good. The best kind of meat is that from lamb, one year old and from suckling kids, but the intestines and the heads are not good. Goats, old cows, and old cheese make bad and heavy food. Poultry meat is more easily digested than the meat of cattle, and the best of poultry is that of the hen. Physicians

say, however, that the food to which man is accustomed is never harmful even if it is bad, because habit becomes second nature, provided he does not eat to excess. . . .

10. A person should eat only when he has a natural desire for food, and not an indulgent desire. A natural desire for food occurs when the stomach is empty; and an indulgent desire is a longing for a particular kind of food. In general, a healthy, strong person should eat twice a day, and the feeble and the aged should eat little at a time, several times during the day, because excessive eating at one time weakens the stomach. He who desires to preserve his physical condition should not eat before his stomach is purged of the previous food. The ordinary length of time for the digestion of food, for people who eat moderately and have moderate exercises, is six hours. It is best to omit one meal during the week, in order that the stomach may have a rest from its work, thus strengthening its digestive power. And it would seem that this omission should take place on Friday.

11. It is advisable that a person should accustom himself to have breakfast in the morning.

12. If one desires to have several kinds of food at one meal, he should first eat the foods which

possess laxative qualities, but he should not mix them with the other food. He should wait a while between the two kinds of food. One should likewise eat first light foods which are easily digested; for instance, fowl meat should be eaten before the meat of cattle, and the meat of small cattle before the meat of big cattle. Food possessing costive qualities should be eaten directly after the meal, and not too much.

Chewing

13. Since the digestive process begins with grinding the food with the teeth and by mixing it with the juice of the saliva, one should not swallow any food without masticating it well, because it will overtax the stomach and make digestion difficult.

Choosing Foods According to the Climate

14. It has already been stated above (section 7) that people differ with respect to their temperaments, and therefore, every person should, on the advice of a physician, choose the food according to his temperament, the climate and the season. In general, the ancient medical scientists have divided foods into various classifications. Some foods are extremely injurious, and it is advisable not to eat them at all, for instance, large stale salted fish, stale salted cheese, mushrooms and

truffles, stale salted meat, wine fresh from the press, cooked food which has lost its flavor, and any kind of food which has a bad odor or a bitter taste; all of these are like deadly poison to the body. There is another class of food which is also injurious, although not as bad as the former; therefore, one should eat little of these and only on rare occasions. One should not become accustomed to eat them as one's steady diet, or even eat a little at every meal. These are: large fish, cheese, milk twenty-four hours after the milking, meat of large oxen or large he-goats, barley bread, unleavened bread, cabbage, leek, onions, garlic, mustard and radishes; all of these are unwholesome, and one should eat very little of them in the winter, but in the summer they should be entirely avoided.

Harmful Foods

15. There are other kinds of food which are unwholesome, but less injurious than the former. They are the following: aquatic fowl, small young pigeons, dates, bread kneaded in oil, and fine flour which has been so thoroughly sifted that even the odor of the bran disappeared. One should not eat too much of these.

16. One should always abstain from eating fruit of the trees, and one should not eat too much of

them even when they are dried, much less before
they are fully ripened on the tree, they are just
like swords to the body. Carobs are always injurious. Pickled fruits are bad, and one should eat
very little of them during the summer or in warm
climates. Figs, grapes, almonds and pomegran-
ates are always wholesome, whether fresh or
dried, and one may eat of them to one's fill. Yet
one must not eat them steadily as one's daily diet,
although they are the most wholesome of all the
fruits.

17. As regards drinking, water is the natural
drink for a person and it is healthful. If the water
is clean and pure, it is helpful in that it preserves
the moisture of the body and hastens the ejection
of waste. One should choose cool water for drinking, because it satisfies the thirst and helps the
digestion more than water which is not cold. But
the water should not be too cold, because it di-
minishes the natural warmth of the body. Especially when a man is tired and weary, he should
be careful not to drink very cold water; because
the fat of the heart at such a time is hot and it
becomes dissolved, and cold water may cause
such harm as to prove fatal, God forbid. Although
water is good for the health, it should not be
drunk to excess. One should drink no water before the meal, because when the stomach be-

comes cooled off, it will not digest the food properly. Only a little water mixed with wine should one drink in the middle of the meal, and only when the food begins to become digested may one drink a moderate portion of water. One should drink no water upon leaving the bath-house, so that the liver may not become cooled off, and surely one should abstain from drinking water while being in the bath-house. Neither should one drink water immediately after having sexual intercourse, because the natural warmth of the body is then weakened, and it may cause paralysis of the limbs.

18. Wine preserves the natural warmth of the body, improves digestion, helps the expulsion of waste, and is good for the health, provided it is used moderately. A person who suffers from headaches should abstain from drinking wine, because it fills the head with gases and may aggravate this condition. Wine is good for the aged but injurious to the young, because it increases the warmth of the body, and it is like adding fuel to fire. It is advisable for one to abstain from wine up to the age of twenty-one. A little wine should be drunk before the meal, in order to open up the intestines. Wine should not be drunk when hungry, or after a bath, or after perspiring, or while being tired and weary. It should be drunk sparingly during meals.

When to Eat

19. A person should eat only when he is hungry, and drink when he is thirsty, and should not neglect the call of nature even for one moment, and should not begin consuming food before he ascertains whether he has an urge to purge.

20. A man should ever endeavor to keep his bowels lax, even approaching a diarrhetic state; for this is a leading rule in hygiene, that as long as the bowels are constipated or when they act with difficulty, serious diseases may result. Therefore, when a person observes that his bowels do not function properly, he should consult a physician.

21. Toil in a moderate degree is good for the physical health, but excessive toil, as well as idleness, are injurious to the body. In the hot season, a little exercise will suffice, but in the cold season, more is required. A fat person requires more exercise than a lean person.

Psychosomatization

22. One who desires to preserve his health must learn about his psychological reactions and control them; joy, worry, anger and fright are psychological reactions. A wise man must always be satisfied with his portion during the time of his vain existence, and should not grieve over a world

that does not belong to him. He should not look for luxuries, and he should be in good spirits and joyous to a moderate extent at all times, because these characteristics help increase the natural warmth of the body, to digest the food, to eliminate the superfluous matter, to strengthen the eyesight and the other faculties, and to strengthen the power of reasoning. But one should not try to stimulate the joy of life by means of eating or drinking, as the fools do, for the reason that by too much joy, the warmth of the heart is diffused over the entire body, and the natural warmth of the heart is cooled off, with the result that it may cause sudden death. Especially can that happen to fat persons, because the natural warmth in their bodies is little, for the reason that the blood vessels in their bodies are narrow, and the circulation of the blood, which is the main cause of the warmth, is slow. Grief, which is the reverse of joy, is likewise injurious, because it cools off the body and the natural warmth centralizes into the heart, which condition may cause death. Anger stirs up the warmth of the body, so that it produces a kind of fever. Fright causes coolness in the body and therefore, it happens that the frightened person begins to shiver, and when the coolness increases, it may cause death. And how much more must one take care not to eat when angry, frightened, or worried, but eat when only moderately happy.

Sleep and Nutrition

23. Moderate sleep is good for the physical well-being, because it helps digest food and rest the senses; and if one is unable to sleep because of illness, one should eat such foods that stimulate sleep. Too much sleep, however, is injurious, because it increases the gases that come up from the belly, fills up the head with them, and causes serious harm to the body. Just as one must be careful not to sleep immediately after eating, so must one take care not to go to sleep when one is hungry, because when there is no food in the body, the natural warmth works in the superfluous matter producing foul gases which enter the head. When sleeping, the head should be higher than the rest of the body, because it will help the food come down from the stomach, and it will diminish the gases that come up into the head. The natural sleep is the one at night; sleep in the daytime is harmful, and is good only for those who are accustomed to it.

24. The proper way of washing oneself is to take a bath regularly every week. One should not enter the bath-house when one is either hungry or full, but when the food is beginning to become digested. One should wash the body with hot water, afterward with tepid water, then with water some degrees cooler, and finally with cold water. Upon

leaving the bath-house, one should put on one's clothes and cover the head well, thereby avoiding catching a cold; it is necessary to take this precaution even in the summer time. One should not eat immediately upon leaving the bath-house, but one should wait until one regains his mental and physical composure, and allow the heat to subside, and then eat. If one can take a nap upon leaving the bath-house, before his meal, so much the better.

Pollution

25. A person should endeavor to dwell where the air is pure and clear, on elevated ground, and in a house of ample proportions. If possible, he should not dwell in a house having either a northern or an eastern exposure, and there should be no decayed matter around. It is very beneficial to continually purify the air of the house with fragrant substances and by proper fumigation.

26. The air best for the physical well-being is that of even temperature, neither too hot nor too cold. Therefore, precautions should be taken not to overheat the house in the winter as many senseless people do, because excessive heat occasions many illnesses, God forbid. A house should be heated just enough so that the cold should not be felt, but it should not be too hot.

Vision

27. To preserve one's eyesight, one should guard against the following: not to enter suddenly from a dark place into a well-illuminated place. He should first open the door of the well-lighted room slightly, and look at that dim light for a moment, then open it a little more, and finally open it completely. One should also take the same precaution when coming from a well-lighted place into a dark one. The change from light to darkness and from darkness to light, without a medium, is injurious to the eyesight. Therefore, the Holy One, blessed be His name, has in His mercy so created the world that the sun should begin shining upon the earth gradually, not at once, and so does it set gradually. On account of this, we say the benediction *Hammeir laaretz veladarim aleha berahamim* (Who in mercy giveth light to the earth and to them that dwell thereon); which means, that in His mercy He gives us light gradually and not suddenly, at once. The light that is reflected from the light of the sun, that is, when the sun shines down on some place and from there the light is reflected, is very injurious to the eyes. Therefore, one should not dwell in a house, the windows of which face to the north only, because the sun never shines from the north, and whatever light there is in such house is obtained only by reflec-

tion. Even if the windows face east, south or west, but if the open sky cannot be seen through them, being obstructed by high walls, the light that penetrates through them is likewise only a reflection. One should not write, read, or do any delicate work in the dusk of twilight, nor in the middle of the day when the sun shines the brightest. Neither should one write or read too much small print nor do any delicate work before candle light at night. Gazing steadily at a white color is likewise harmful to the eyes; therefore is the color of the sky blue, not white, in order not to hurt the eyes. Gazing steadily at bright red colors or at fire is also injurious. Smoke, sulphurous odors, fine dust and strong wind blowing in the face, excessive or rapid walking, and excessive weeping are injurious to the eyes; for it is written (Lamentations 2:11): "My eyes do fail with tears." The most injurious of all is excessive copulation; but "The precept of the Lord is pure, enlightening the eyes" (Psalms 19:9).

5

THE GREAT BANQUET

Nutrition and *sustenance* are two inseparable words. In a broad sense, the idea of sustaining oneself relates to fulfilling basic needs of various kinds. But sustaining oneself with food remains the primary sense of this word.

Eating is clearly the main obligation of living beings. We don't have to do anything to take in oxygen, since that is accomplished by an automatic, involuntary process. We have no direct influence on our genetic health, either. Eating—whether by hunting, harvesting, or other means—is the universal job of all creatures. Sustenance derives from this primary need but is not limited to it. Throughout their development, human beings have considered as sustenance anything that allays hunger, and not in the nutritional sense only. And how hungry might an individual get? Could hunger be insatiable?

Our organism is limited. Therefore, hunger that is greater than the need for food leads to obesity. Each and every person must regulate his or her hunger according to his or her capacity to absorb. And we must all try to adjust our hunger not only for food but for livelihood, sex, and other needs. Pleasure arises from the perfect regulation of these desires. The more food, livelihood, and sex one absorbs, the more satiated, obese, and bored one becomes, thus turning pleasure into suffering.

An outstanding definition of correlations between nourishment and sustenance, hunger and need, is brought to light by the Kabbalist Rabbi Nathan[56] when he discusses the manna given by God to sustain the Jewish people in the wilderness after their Exodus from Egypt. Rabbi Nathan concentrates on the fact that these were controlled daily portions. He writes:

> The sustenance of a person can be symbolized by the idea of the manna. In its deepest meaning, manna (or sustenance) originates from the most hidden supernal planes, as it is written: ". . . for they did not know what it was" (Exodus 16:15). The manna represents the most difficult test to human beings, since to have access to it, they have to go through the most "filthy places." This is so because one's daily sustenance originates in a very recondite and exalted source, and the moment it penetrates this material world, its original light becomes immediately concealed. For such light cannot be apprehended in a rational way, but through faith only. Therefore, the instant when the manna came down from Heaven for

daily sustenance, it was difficult for the people to believe it would also come on the following day. Such doubt constantly assaults the heart. And because they did not believe the manna would come on the following day, many of the people started storing part of their manna for the next morning, and "it became putrid and maggoty with worms" (Exodus 16:20). The truth is that the manna for a specific day serves for that day alone.[57]

Rabbi Nathan writes about this immoderate hunger as being caused by lack of faith. We may define faith as trust or certainty in the chain of receiving. The Sea of Galilee allows the melted snows to flow freely and does not hold on to them; it does not question whether the waters that it releases will ever be replaced.

If the appetite, both literally and figuratively, is not regulated, we face the risk of "getting less" or "retaining more" than we should. Since the latter is the main focus of our interest, namely "obesity," it must be stressed that a diet will never work unless we start paying attention to the entire process of our sustenance. An overconcern with sustenance, for example, indicates insecurity and lack of trust. And the less we trust, the more we retain. Those who retain get too fat, and those who get too fat lead an unbalanced life.

There is a limited potential for receiving and giving that varies from one person to the next. If we concern ourselves only with our due portion, our manna for today, we are sure to get our share for tomorrow. But it will be guaranteed only if today's hunger is real. One may receive tomorrow's portion, but one will lose the right to the guarantee. Satiation is then transformed into suffering; with every mouthful comes the doubt: What am I going to live on tomorrow? This is valid both for the individual in relation to society and for a group of individuals in relation to their ecosystem.

Hunger is, therefore, insatiable when it is not a true hunger, when it misses the connection with real needs. Before beginning the life banquet, it is worth asking what true hunger is, because food will never run out for a true hunger. "Those who turn to the Lord shall not lack any good"(Psalms 34:11).

6

HUNGER AND HEALTH
IN THE NEXT WORLD

For the Jews, the orally oriented people, what better way to describe life after death, the World to Come (*Olam ha-Ba*), than as a great banquet, the quintessential banquet. According to Jewish tradition, the tzaddikim will be attending this banquet in the Olam ha-Ba, each receiving according to his or her own capacity. They will be seated in such a way that those who have done better will be closer to the head of the table, where sits the great throne and on it the Holy Glutton, blessed be He.

My words will sound irreverent unless you understand what banquet, what food, and what appetite we are talking about. In reality, everyone has some difficulty understanding what the World to Come is. The symbolism expressed by laid tables and banquets is designed to aid our understanding. But of course we are not trying to comprehend what the afterlife is, for that effort would be in vain. We are only trying to gain an understanding of the

World to Come so that we can better live in this world of here and now. One speculates on death in order to better understand life.

In this book I have tried to clarify the understanding of "diet" as a way of being in harmony with life. The performance of the digestive system, which begins with the rain falling over the fields (or even before), finishes (although it is never really complete) with human consciousness. To our best knowledge, this consciousness is the most sophisticated form of self-awareness on the entire planet, and it cannot be fully accomplished if it is dissociated from the larger chain of exchanges around it. The dissociation of consciousness from the flow of exchanges in the universe fattens us and everything else.

In the broader sense, the World to Come does not mean a discontinuity from life itself. It will only be a discontinuity if we eat—that is, partake of the life banquet, the laid table—in a way that is disconnected from life. In that case, aiming exclusively at storing, at receiving and retaining as an end in itself, we become fat and get in the way of life's digestion.

By discontinuity from life, I do not mean punishment of any kind, purgatories or hells. It is not the World to Come that represents a separation from life but rather the present world that can be experienced as such. The best description of hell is not as an imaginary world somewhere else, but as a hellish experience of daily life situations, occurrences, or relationships. Here the secret is revealed: The Great Banquet is not reserved for the hereafter but has already begun! In fact, it probably never began nor ceased to exist—this eternal buffet maintained by the ultimate *Chef de Cuisine*, Who attends with care to every detail, from the aperitif to the *pièce de résistance* and the dessert.

Will we, then, behave the same in the World to Come as we do here? Yes, for if we do and live the banquet accordingly, by dieting in a physical, emotional, intellectual, and spiritual way, there is no discontinuity. And that is exactly what the rabbis want to stress. In this future world, people not only feast but also study. Not that they necessarily eat food made of material substances or study specific subjects; but they still feed themselves from all sources of the universe and continue to learn and understand. Not that they have cutlery or books, but they still help themselves from the banquet as we do and are bound up in the bond of life. Surely there are no restaurants or academies, but there are still menus of possibilities for sharing, exchanging, and learning. And so it is explained in the work *Kedushat ha-Levi:*

> One should not expect the ordinary person to have holy thoughts while eating. For him, a meal in the World to Come will be a real meal, consisting of the finest and most elaborate delicacies and

wines. But the tzaddikim—who relish not food as
such but their holy thoughts over the meals—will
be rewarded with a feast consisting of divine mysteries, which their souls will then fully understand, with no obstacles whatsoever.[58]

In this world, holy people feed on an energy that
has to do not only with material nutritional power, but
also with a total and ideal exchange. In other words, for
the tzaddikim—and there is an inner tzaddik in every
one of us—there is no discontinuity between this world
and the World to Come: they will do in that world just
what they did in this one.

And exactly because there is no separation, the
rabbis say: *Pay attention here and now!* The banquet
proceeds, and we do not have to wait for dessert. Everything on the table is constantly refreshed and replaced,
even that much-longed-for chocolate cake, which seems
unmistakably finite. Here, in this world, the Great Banquet is itself the Great Health—health in all different
aspects of reality.

The life process is more than life itself, for, if we
know how to keep its commandments, our horizons—
now limited to finite pies—expand. The Bible (Deuteronomy 11:13–17) reads:

If you are careful to pay heed to My commandments, which I am prescribing to you today, and

if you love God your Lord with all your heart and soul [then God has made this promise]: I will grant the fall and spring rains in your land at their proper time, so that you will have an ample harvest of grain, oil, and wine. I will grant forage in your fields for your animals; and you will eat and be satisfied.

Be careful that your heart not be tempted to go astray and worship other gods, bowing down to them. God's anger will then be directed against you, and He will lock up the skies so that there will not be any rain. The land will not give forth its crops, and you will rapidly vanish from the good land that God is giving you.

Life itself is a Great Diet. It is not by chance that "in the beginning was the mouth"—the potential tool for this endless give-and-take of the universe with itself. Maybe we can learn with the tzaddik, image and likeness of the Great Tzaddik, Who can eat but not merely eat; Who can entirely engage in the constant flow of exchange that ever was, ever is, and ever will be.

Notes

1. Adapted from *The Complete ArtScroll Siddur* (Brooklyn, N.Y.: Mesorah Publications, 1987).
2. Vowels are not considered part of the stem in Hebrew words. This accounts for leaving out the letters A and E.
3. *Shulḥan Arukh* is the title of the most popular Jewish code of rabbinic laws. It was written by Joseph Caro in the sixteenth century with the aim of making the law more accessible to the layperson by presenting a concise collection of rabbinical decisions on laws and customs.
4. The chief disciple of Rabbi Isaac Luria (see note 6), Ḥayyim Vital (1543–1620), from Safed, Israel, developed his master's thought and recorded it in writing.
5. Hasidism accepts joy and mysticism as part of Jewish religious life. Mainly directed to illiterate and poor audiences, the movement was based on the relationship of the rabbis (rebbes) and their followers, and storytelling was the main technique for transmitting teachings.
6. The Lurianic Kabbalah was developed by Rabbi Isaac Luria (1534–1572), known as the Ari, regarded by many as the greatest Kabbalists of all times. He went to the heart of the primary kabbalistic concepts and produced a vast and sophisticated philosophical system.

7. Paraphrased from Louis Jacobs, "Eating as an Act of Worship" (1982), p. 8.

8. A disciple of the Rebbe of Mezeritch, Rabbi Levi Isaac of Berdichev (1740–1809) was known as the Berdichever Rabbi.

9. A disciple of the Maggid of Mezeritch, Rabbi Shneur Zalman of Liadi (1813) was known as the Liadier.

10. The renowned American rabbi (1925–1994), known as the Singing Rabbi. He is considered the most important contemporary composer of popular religious songs.

11. A disciple of the Lubliner Rabbi, Reb Simḥa Bunam from Pshiskhe (1765–1827) was known as the Yud, "the Jew."

12. In J. Kleiman, ed., *Niflaot ha-Yehudi* (in Yiddish) (Warsaw, 1925).

13. In C. Yedvobner, ed., *Shaar Bat Rabim* (in Hebrew) (Bialistok, 1914), p. 16.

14. J. K. K. Rokotz, ed., *Tiferet ha-Yehudi* (in Hebrew) (Warsaw, 1911).

15. L. Newman, *The Hasidic Anthology* (New York: Schocken Books, 1963), p. 100:11.

16. A disciple of the Baal Shem Tov, Reb Dov Baer (1710–1772) was known as the Maggid (Storyteller or Preacher) of Mezeritch.

17. L. Abraham, ed. *Midrash Ribesh Tov*, II (in Hebrew), 5th ed. (Kecskemet, 1927).

18. This example is paraphrased from his comments in a lecture delivered in San Francisco, 1982.

19. *Shabbat* 105b.

20. A disciple of the Baal Shem Tov, Rabbi Yeḥiel Mikhel (d. 1781) of Zlotchov was known as the Zlotchover.

21. A disciple of Reb Bunam, Rabbi Isaac of Vorka (1779–1848) was known as the Vorker.
22. Martin Buber, *Die chassidischen Bücher* (Berlin, 1928), p. 548.
23. Ibid., p. 417.
24. A. Kaham, ed., *Kedushat Eliezer* (in Yiddish) (Warsaw, 1930), p. 74.
25. M. S. Kleinman, ed., *Or Yesharim* (in Hebrew) (Piotrkow, 1924), p. 108.
26. E. Bergman, ed., *Kotzer Ma'asiot* (in Yiddish) (Warsaw, 1924), p. 41.
27. *Pirkei Avot* 1:14.
28. A disciple of the Mezeritcher Rabbi, Rabbi Shlomo (d. 1792) was known as the Kaliner.
29. Y. A. Kamelhan, ed., *Dor De'ah*, (in Hebrew) (Bilguraj, 1933), p. 170.
30. *Shaarei Ruaḥ ha-Kodesh* (Gates to the Holy Spirit). Compiled by Rabbi Vital in the sixteenth century and first published in 1863, this anthology of eight books ("gates") includes most of the Ari's teachings.
31. Kleinman, *Or Yesharim*, p. 31.
32. *Shabbat* 88a.
33. *Sanhedrin* 59b.
34. *Ḥullin* 84a.
35. S. Y. Agnon, "Tears," translated by Jules Harlow (New York: Schocken Books, 1966).
36. Martin Buber, *Die Erzählungen der Chassidim*, 1946.
37. *Berakhot*, 50b
38. Martin Buber, *Ten Rungs: Hasidic Sayings* (New York: Schocken Books, 1947).

NOTES

39. Newman, *The Hasidic Anthology*, p. 113:8.
40. Ibid.
41. *Avot de Rabbi Natan*, 26.
42. Philo, *Quod deterius potiori insidiari soleat* (That the Worse Attacks the Better), chap. 1.
43. The first-century sage Hillel was the first rabbi to codify the oral law. He constantly debated with another renowned master, Shammai. Both men were known among the *zugot* (students paired together for the purpose of debating).
44. *Leviticus Rabbah* 34:3.
45. S. Breitstein, *Simhat Israel* (in Hebrew) (Piotrkow, 1910), p. 72.
46. "Preserving Youth," *Mishneh Torah*.
47. A disciple of the Baal Shem Tov, Reb Pinhas Shapiro (1791) was known as the Koretzer.
48. The sage Ben Sira (170 BCE), also known as Simeon ben Sirach, was a scribe and the author of *The Wisdom of Ben Sira* and other works.
49. *The Wisdom of Ben Sira*, 21: 12–20.
50. From Ben-Meir's commentary on *Pesahim* 113a.
51. *The Kabbalah of Money* (Boston & London: Shambhala Publications, 1996) was the first book of my trilogy (consisting of *The Kabbalah of Money*, *The Kabbalah of Food*, and *The Kabbalah of Envy*) to be published in English.
52. Rabbi Nahman of Bratslav, *Likutei Moharan* (New York: Bratslaver Press, 1992).
53. Bergman, *Kotzer Maasiot*, p. 18.
54. Hyman E. Goldin, trans., *Kitzur Shulhan Aruh* (Brooklyn: Hebrew Publication Co., 1961), Vol. 1, pp. 101–108. Reprinted with permission.

55. *Nutarikin,* or *notarikon,* is a kabbalistic technique (already referred to in chapter 2) for interpreting the Torah. It entails abbreviating or reversing the letters of Hebrew words. (The Hebrew letters contained in Goldin's translation of the Kitzur have been omitted from the extract, and the words have been transliterated.)

56. A disciple of Naḥman of Bratslav, Rabbi Nathan unveiled secrets about his master in *Likutei Halaḥot.*

57. In *Likutim* (New York: Bratslaver Press, 1992), p. 200.

58. In *Likutim,* p. 288.

Bibliography

Ben Amos & Mintz. *In Praise of the Baal Shem Tov.* Bloomington, IN: Indiana University Press, 1980.

Buber, Martin. *Histórias do Rabi.* São Paulo: Perspectiva, 1967.

————. *Ten Rungs: Hasidic Sayings.* New York: Schocken Books, 1947.

Dresner, S. *The Zaddik.* New York: Schocken Books, 1960.

Green, Arthur. *Tormented Master.* New York: Schocken Books, 1981.

Houston, Jean. *The Search for the Beloved.* New York: St. Martin's Press, 1982.

Jimenez, J. R. *God Desired and Desiring.* New York: Paragon House, 1987.

Kadushin, M. *The Rabbinic Mind.* New York: Bloch, 1952.

Kaplan, Aryeh. *Meditation and Kabbalah.* York Beach, Maine: Samuel Weiser, 1982.

————, trans. *The Living Torah: The Five Books of Moses and the Haftarot.* New York: Maznaim, 1981.

Klagsbrun, F. *Voices of Wisdom.* New York: Pantheon, 1980.

Nahman of Breslov, Rabbi. *Ayeh.* Brooklyn, N.Y.: Breslov Research Institute, 1985.

Newman, L. *The Hasidic Anthology.* New York: Schocken Books, 1963.

BIBLIOGRAPHY

Roskies, D. *Against the Apocalypse.* Cambridge: Harvard University Press, 1984.

Siegel, D. *Where Heaven and Earth Touch.* New York: Town House Press, 1983.

Siegel, D., Strassfeld & Strassfeld. *The Jewish Catalog.* New York: Schocken Books, 1977.

Sladovnik, M., ed. *Maasiot ha-Gedolim Ḥadash.* Warsaw, 1925.

Printed in the United States
by Baker & Taylor Publisher Services